AROUND THE PALMA SOLA LOOP

with Fred Hall

illustrated by Robt Hall

Copyright 1986 by Fred Hall

ISBN 0-8200-1033-2

Acknowledgments

My wife, Kathryn Lang Hall, deserves special thanks for her encouragement, patience and help while I struggled through reams of longhand. Linda Hall Perez, my niece, was most liberal with her special talent of "talk typing", a service that permitted me to complete this manuscript. My son, Robert Miller Hall, a professor of art in St. Augustine, visited locations with me to provide the illustrations for the text and cover. This book is more of a family affair than an individual effort. I express my appreciation to the few old timers who visited and talked with me about the people and life in old Palma Sola during the 1915 to 1920 period.

Fred L Hall

Published By:

The GREAT OUTDOORS PUBLISHING COMPANY

4747-28th Street North
St. Petersburg, FL 33714

Preface

The times, the travel, the adventure, the comedy, the tragedy that I have encountered in the past seventy odd years has not erased the impressions that were made on my inquisitive and alert young mind while living in Old Palma Sola. I was entranced by the strange beauty of the area and the new, to me, way of community life during the period just prior to and after World War I.

An abrupt change in environment caused by my family's move from the arid southeastern high desert and mountains in the territory of Arizona caused me to be transplanted into a beautiful, mysterious, and most intriguing land. Our life in Arizona had not been unpleasant, the family's fortunes had been adequate to keep up with the Joneses. Florida people, with different food, habits and ways, with speech and vocabulary strangeness, plus an abundance of green growth and water, to me seemed a miraculous change, all for the better.

A teenager, by nature, feels the urge to explore the other side of the mountain, thus my curiosity was continually challenged by strange customs, the nature of the people and the mysteries of the land.

Barefooted, I trod sand ruts and trails, through the woods, in darkness and daylight, to and from the groves, fields or docks, in pursuit of work or play, my mind exploring the areas behind lighted windows, inventing or imagining conversations, dreaming of exploits.

As I gazed into the star-studded heavens at night, I prayed that I would be loved by all, and someday become a drummer and make one hundred dollars a month, so that I could help out my Mother and Dad, drive a car, and take my girl to the Wallace Theater in "Bradentown" on Saturday night.

During the past seventy years I have, at intervals, had the opportunity to visit Palma Sola and travel around the old Loop Road again.

Now I erase the modern and search the archives of my mind for the impressions so firmly implanted during the 1915-1920 period, which I will endeavor to record as I saw and felt them at that time.

Truth or fiction, take your choice, as I have had to do in my effort to record something of the life and the people of Old Palma Sola. Truly a most unique community, composed of high pine woods, swamps, hammocks, salt flats, marshes, rivershore, bayous and bays, and an amalgamation of souls with a truly live and let live conscience, a wide variety of desirable and practical talents, with a live off the land and sea ability, plus a real compassion for others, whether or not deserved.

Chapter I

Hop's Store and Post Office

A most unusual bit of geography located in Manatee County, Florida, was, in the early 1880's, named Palma Sola, and took in all lands west of Warner's Bayou west fork, between the Manatee River and Palma Sola Bay, extending west to Perico Bayou. All lands east of Warner's Bayou along the Manatee River, extending to Sarasota Avenue (now Bradenton's 26th Street W.) was Fogartyville, with its own general store, commercial dock, and post office.

"Bradentown" was the county seat of Manatee County, which at that time included Sarasota, Venice, and the Keys—beaches and backwoods, south almost to Punta Gorda.

Around the Palma Sola Loop

Most Palma Sola families considered the trip into Bradenton a monthly or even a semi-annual excursion, unless there was an election or a hanging.

Tampa and St. Petersburg were so remote to many Palma Solians that they were only imaginary places.

The old Palma Sola community really started where the shell road, called Riverview Boulevard, came to a dead-end at the east Loop Road. The area to the west was woods. East of the north-south road, cornering on Riverview Boulevard, some brave soul had built two cement block buildings, both two-story. The corner building contained the Palma Sola Post Office and a general store on the ground floor. The second floor was reached by an outside wooden stairway, and consisted of several small sparsely furnished rooms for rent. Water was obtained from a pitcher pump in the yard back of the store, where a path through the sand spurs led to a three-holer under a spruce pine in the white sand area where hole digging was easy.

The store was operated by one Hop Drawdy, who was also Postmaster. The store enjoyed two rush hours, one when the mail arrived by horse and buggy from Bradenton, with a stopover at the Fogertyville store and post office. The mailman's arrival could be expected about noon. Another rush hour occurred after sundown, except in the long summer days, when the male population, ages twelve and up, began to show up well before sundown, to sit on the counters and chairs, maybe spend a dime in good times for a bottle of pop and some cheese and crackers, and unlike the West, where a sack of Bull Durham and free papers made up a smoke, Prince Albert in a pipe or rolled into a fat cigarette, pleased those who were not chewing their favorite Apple sun-cured or natural leaf. Chewing meant frequent trips to the outside door—Hop just wouldn't stand for spitting in the corners.

Now this Hop was a native of the Florida east coast. How he came to settle in Palma Sola and acquire the few dollars to start the store, as well as being appointed Postmaster, had an air of mystery. His wife was a native Conch, with all of the characteristics of her Key West origin. Also, she was several years younger than Hop. The Drawdy family lived next door to the store in the two-story block building with the front porch,

Hop's Store and Post Office

and took care of the roomers in both buildings. Mrs. Hop was seen in the store only at rare intervals, sticking her head in the door with a message or demand for Hop, and occasionally to tend the Post Office in an emergency. She was a pleasant, typical Conch, usually with a child straddling her hip, and always supported by one or two of her Key West kin folk, who seemed to be perpetual visitors.

Born with a club foot, thus the nickname Hop, this 5 foot 10 inch crackerboy grew into manhood tending woods cattle, grinding cane, penning razorback hogs and attending a two-room country school, and, of course, never missing the annual revivals, usually Holy-Roller, that were a part of backwoods Florida life. This raising was a pretty good preparation, necessary for him to meet most of life's trials and tribulations, and at the store, to act as judge, jury, defense and prosecution, when the opinions and ideas of the assembled men and boys, "can read, can't read" corner store gathering was in session.

The mail time gatherings were composed mostly of men not engaged in fishing, farm or grove work, mostly oldies, younger boys, seldom any girls, and a few ladies who justified their presence by purchasing a bag of grits, some white meat, a spool of thread or a filling of the one gallon kerosene lamp oil can. Some of the men and women were even addressed as Mister or Misses, but it was mostly just Uncle and Aunt. Much of the community's gossip, news, politics and hear-say originated at the Post Office, then covered the entire Palma Sola Loop area like the dew.

The evening group at the store, 100% male, was often dignified by the attendance of the Evans brothers, James and "Tubby" Hershel who owned their own celery farm and camped out in a shack on the farm during the celery growing season, while their families enjoyed city life in Bradenton. Then there was Wilbur Sikes, who never or seldom worked out, but always seemed to be able to jingle coins in his pocket. The Pillsbury boys, the Davises, the Pettigrews, the Smiths, the Warners, the Felts, the Phelps, and the Rogers were permanents, supported either by fishing, fruit groves, truck farming on their own land, or working in the jelly factory, while the Coopers, the Halls, the Pierces, the Shipmans and half a dozen others, were either sharecroppers or just plain hungry field hands.

The patriarch of this group was Capt. Charley Davis, a heavy mustachioed father of a large family, housed in a ramshackled board and batten weather-beaten house down by the river, where the net spreads, mullet smoke house and a thrown together shelter-shack to house the various boat building tools and fishing gear trailed out from the house along the high tide line into the mangroves. The sand hill bluff where the house sat was, fortunately, several feet above high tide line. The plot supported several citrus and guava trees, a mango and a sapadillo, and a few chickens roosted in the trees and nested in a box under a guava tree. None of Capt. Davis' family planted a seed, gardening was just not their thing, but night or day it was all the same—no regular time for meals, sleep or fishing—but the elusive pompano seemed to favor the nets of Capt. Davis' boys, and the Davis smoked mullet was favored by all. The infrequently smoked batches were immediately consumed, while the local gentry awaited news of another batch from the smoker, for only the fat, prime, freshly dressed fish entered Capt. Davis' smokehouse, which was fired with buttonwood, properly known as black mangrove.

Capt. Davis did not do much talking at the store. His ability to listen to all and sundry, without comment, may have been due to a family condition, for after the birth of his five children Aunt Mary Davis, his wife, became the housekeeper for a Tampa doctor. The oldest daughter went into nurses training, the oldest boy went to sea. Aunt Mary came down to Palma Sola on the steamer two or three times a year. Alma, the second daughter, kept the house. The next older boy, Asa, a Beau Brummel, did some fishing. The younger boy, Earl, nicknamed "Precious", was still in school. Capt. Davis sat around the kitchen stove, fired by driftwood in the fall and winter. The kitchen was small, the coffee pot on the stove never empty or fresh. Spring and summer, while not at the store or smoking fish, Capt. Davis sat in the shade of the mangroves by the net spread. He was never known to sleep in a bed or remove his stiff collar. He wore a jacket when all others were in shirt sleeves, but somehow always looked clean and fresh. Some folks said he landed in Palma Sola at the Shaw's Point Pirate

Hop's Store and Post Office

Spring aboard a Spanish smack as a prisoner and managed to stay ashore when the smack sailed off. Another story is that he had been a captain of a Carolina schooner that had been pirated, which seemed more appropriate. Somehow he made his way to Palma Sola, married Mary Bishop of the early pioneer Bishop family, settled down, built a board and batten four room cottage on the sand bluff at Bishop Point, and lived by fishing, small boat building and net knitting.

The Wednesday evening gathering at Hop's store drew a larger group. Some of the regulars did not show up, but the Wednesday-only attendants more than made up the difference, for this was the night that Hop read from the Bible and asked each one present to pray aloud and alone to teach him to speak out and show his love for God in public. The prayers were varied. The older Evans boy prayed long and loud for the black heart to skip their celery crop that year. Bud Shipman, who cold neither read nor write, was slow and deliberate in his prayer that Nancy, who was bound out to a Yankee family, would work out her bond and return to him pure, but he would take her even if she were with child by some Yankee who had done her wrong. Wilbur Sikes always prayed that Mr. Hull, the Tennessee rich man who owned the two block buildings, would build a hotel in Palma Sola as a fishermen's resort and get the Tampa-Bradenton steamboat to stop at the dock. Several of the prayers consisted of a single Amen, and Hop ended up with a lengthy hardshell Baptist type prayer, asking to be spared from the fires of Hell, and for all of Palma Sola to be forgiven their many sins. One of Hop's never omitted requests was for all to honor the sanctity of the family and to take the virgin only in wedlock. Hop had two daughters, no sons.

Around the Palma Sola Loop

Chapter II

Characters, Customs, Cultures and War

The vacant property west of the store was grubbed and stepped off into a baseball field, cement sacks filled with sand serving as bases. The team was organized by Hop, with Jim Evans as captain. Practice was irregular, seldom were eighteen players available for a real game. The only real competition was once a year with Cortez. This game was always scheduled on a Saturday at low tide as the game was played on the sand flats in Cortez that were flooded at high tide.

The landing dock in Cortez was south of the entrance into Palma Sola Bay, near the west end of Hunters Point where Sarasota Sound was less than one half mile wide.

The Palma Sola team left Grampa Pillsbury's dock in Palma Sola Bay aboard Tommy Adams' fishing boat for the one hour, five mile trip to Cortez. The winning team was awarded a box of twenty-five Tampa Nugget cigars by a Mr. Dowling, who had a store in Cortez. The umpire of these infrequent games was one Jap Thigpen, known as the toughest fisherman in the Cortez area. It was said that he could beat any man in Cortez with one hand in his hip pocket. Never were any of Jap's baseball calls challenged, even when Hop, who had the habit of kicking his club foot out over the plate when at bat, was occasionally hit by the pitched ball. Jap would shout "No base, you are out! Intentionally hit by a pitched ball".

Around the Palma Sola Loop

The Thigpen family was the only resident on Tidy Island. They had a small truck patch, plus the usual net spreads and fishing skiffs, and a skipjack poling boat with a long poling oar—which was the Thigpen's transportation to and from Cortez.

Tidy Island is about a quarter of a mile southeast of Cortez Village. The island was mostly salt flats and marshes, with only about forty acres of the 200 or so total acreage suitable for cultivation.

At this time none of the Palma Sola men or boys had the desire to more than lightly use or sample the 'shine that was known by all to be the livelihood of quite a few families. One particular bachelor, Mr. Engle, forded the shallow bayou to Perico Island where he lived in a shack, tended his still, and kept his horse in a lean-to that seemed in some way to keep his shack from collapsing. His mash barrels and his still were some one hundred yards away from his shack in the dense mangroves. This Mr. Engle also had a legally owned plot and shack in the Pinehurst section near Mrs. Simpson's large two-story rambling house that was set up as Simpson's Orphanage. Mr. Engle always called on Mrs. Simpson on his trips from Perico to Palma Sola to shop for provisions, get his mail, and spend a day or so tending the few pineapple plants, guava and downy myrtles that survived the scant attention on his Pinehurst plot. That call at Mrs. Simpson's Orphanage was probably the real reason for his trips to Pinehurst, for he made no other social contact and was not prone to engage in casual conversation. His transportation was a one horse wagon. The horse never exceeded a slow walk and if you happened to be near his passing and unobserved, you would hear a one way conversation, always with emphasis, expression and sometimes a chuckle. Hop said Mr. Engle's opening statement, upon entering the store, was always the same. "How much is a loaf of bread today?" "Did I get some mail?" His shopping was meager: one loaf of bakery bread, if available, a wedge of rat trap cheese, and two cans of vienna sausage. It was no mystery that Mr. Engle's main supplies came in by boat to his well-concealed landing in the mangroves on Perico Island. He did not peddle his choice 'shine at random—it was picked up by a bootlegger from up the bay, who brought in the necessary ingredients for the next batch, and some groceries, as he picked up the famous Perico Island 'shine, which he cut to 95 proof and sold in razor blade pints, retailed in Tampa and St. Pete. Now, the razor blade pint is thin, looks big broadside, is thick glass and small cavity, twelve to the gallon. But who is choosey when buying a pint of the rare and exceptionally good Perico Island 'shine? It was believed that Mr. Engle added honey to the regular corn grits, sugar and starter that were the basic ingredients for the mash to be distilled into 'shine, because his mash barrels were always covered with honey bees.

Palma Sola had its society and culture. Poverty, schooling, religion, property owner, squatter or sharecropper, it made little or no difference in acceptance into the social and cultural activities of old Palma Sola. The ladies had their WCTU Chapter. The church, served by circuit riding preachers, seldom skipped a Sunday sermon, and the youth had the Christian Endeavor Society each Sunday night, where religion and romance budded.

The WCTU Chapter was the most active in the community affairs for charity and cultural development. Probably six of the twenty odd members had a telephone, many of them on the same line, which meant that the signal was two short, two long rings, or some such combination, different for each phone, but each subscriber heard the rings for every call on the line. This meant that should you be calling someone on your line, you gave Central the number and then hung up until you heard the ring of the subscriber that you were calling, and, of course, the click, click, click of the inquisitive that were listening in. It was not unusual for some of them to chime in with their own remarks. A WCTU meeting or rich news and gossip could reach all members easily, even in one day, or, if interesting enough, within the hour, simply by two or three subscribers relaying the news to one or two parties on each of the lines serving the community. This was not all bad, for when tragedy occurred, like the death of the Bevil infant, the news spread fast. A box was made, the experienced ladies laid out the body, the bay rum was secured, the grave opened, and, if no parson was available, Deacon Rogers would say the last words. In such cases, for child or adult, it was always Bert Warner, a

Around the Palma Sola Loop

carpenter, with Deacon Rogers and Uncle Jim Felts, who made the casket. Katie Smith, Lillie Hall, and the Rogers girls padded and lined the box, while Carlyle Rogers and Tommy Adams opened the grave.

Grampa Pillsbury had donated the land for church, school and cemetery, so at the time of death in old Palma Sola, the good ladies of the WCTU and their men took care of things. The only cash required was for the bay rum that was used in the coffin, and seldom did anyone know who supplied it.

Cortez had no cemetery as the land was low and flat, and any hole in the ground more than 2 feet deep immediately filled with water. Deaths there were handled much the same as in Palma Sola. A home-made casket was placed on the net table in the stern of a fishing boat. A funeral procession consisted of fishing boats carrying the mourners, pallbearers and friends across Palma Sola Bay. When the boats arrived at Grampa Pillsbury's dock, the pallbearers carried the casket up the narrow dock, where Deacon Roger's wagon, pulled by his mule, Tipperary, waited to complete the trip up the sand ruts to the cemetery.

Palma Sola was favored by the Manatee County School Board. A new, modern, two-room brick school house was built on the land donated by Grampa Pillsbury for this purpose. Also, the County shelled the two outside wheel ruts on the road, leaving the center rut nice soft sand where the horse or mule traveled. This meant that automobiles must select an area where sod or firm dirt existed, for turning out of the shell ruts where there was no sod meant "stuck-in-the-sand." Therefore, the accommodating wagon or buggy driver would usually pull completely out of the road and stop, allowing the automobile to proceed without leaving the two shelled ruts.

The school was also provided with a very modern privy, a long, narrow, two section structure built of brick. The floor was some three feet above ground level and a four holer was designed on each side of the center partition. At one end of the structure, at ground level, a steel door was installed. At the opposite end a brick flue was built. About twice each year old man Kelly was hired to bring in a load of liter wood, which was placed in the catch area under the holes. The wooden board with the large and small seat holes was removed. The open space connecting the seating area to the catch area was closed off and the liter wood ignited. Thus an incinerator was put into action and a fresh start at the privy was established.

Liter wood is the heart of the long leaf turpentine pine, when seasoned, about 70% resin, easily ignited, burns hot and long, and produces a heavy soot.

The water supply at the school came from a driven well in the yard, with a pitcher pump that had to be primed when the pump was not operated for half an hour or so. Thus a priming bucket had to be maintained at the pump site. The fairly cool, brownish water was dipped from the water bucket with a long handled dipper and poured into a cup, can, or whatever drinking receptacle each student was supposed to hold for private use. Playing with the pump was a "no-no"; however, hand and barefoot washing, or your head under the spout, was permitted, if it did not appear to be a game.

The pre-World War I teacher was Miss Amorette Hawley, a sour old maid, who had two seventh grade girls whom she appointed as teacher's aides. They reported all violations in the schoolroom or playground. Usually the teacher applied a switch with vigor and welt-producing strokes to boys only on the sole word of one of these teacher's pets. Most of the parents had a rule: Get switched at school, get another at home. So the welt marks were concealed and no home reports were, in most cases, ever made. Switch welts on the back of some of the boys would, by today's standards, put the teacher in jail for child abuse. Fred Hall had to sleep on his stomach and avoid removing his shirt at home for weeks because of bloody marks and welts he received for calling Bertha Rude a teacher's pet. Fred then dropped out of school, went on the bum, working in the fields, packing houses or boats, sleeping or eating if and when convenient. In those days a boy big enough could find food and shelter, if he would work. Few, if any questions were asked.

Community events, excepting church and WCTU, seldom included other than the youth and young adults. The Christian Endeavor would plan a clam chowder party. A location would be selected at someone's yard, with the use of the kitchen, where water and light were available. Johnny Adams, with a volunteer, dug the big, fat clams from Palma Sola Bay and delivered them to the chowder party location. When the

Around the Palma Sola Loop

clams were opened, all of the broth was saved, and it was hoped that there would be a meat grinder available to grind the clams in the kitchen. Most everyone in those days had a hand operated grinder that would clamp to the table edge. The clams from Palma Sola Bay deep water were giant Cohogs. Johnny Adams, who harvested some commercially, called the big ones Three-To-The-Quart, as he shucked them out and sold them in quart jars.

The chowder was cooked in a big, black, cast iron pot. The girls had diced white meat (salt pork), chopped the onions, peeled the potatoes, and some of the men folk had brought in liter wood for the fire. One of the girls usually took the responsibility of bossing the chowder pot, but the procedure was always the same: clean the pot, boil the salt pork until transparent, pour off the salty water, brown the pork in the pot, then slow down the fire and brown the onions in the pork fat, add the potatoes with just enough water to cover. Slowly cook the potatoes until barely done, no bones, cool the liquid to a slow simmer, add two cans of diluted Pet milk, stir, flash the fire, and the moment the pot starts to boil, add the chopped clams and the broth. I mean lots of clams, no less than 50% of the whole volume. Now the moment the chowder starts to boil, pull the fire so the chowder will not curdle and the clams will stay tender, then ladle this chowder out into whatever serving dishes, cups, etc., are available, and devour with soda crackers or cold cornbread. You will remember the rich clam flavor forever and ever.

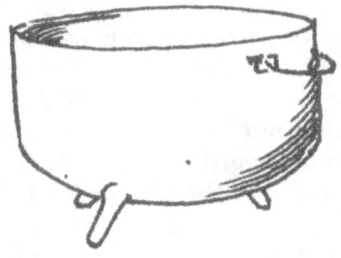

Chowder pot

The chicken pileau parties were about the same as far as planning and preparation went. Capt. Charlie Davis, or some other patriarch, usually donated a couple of old hens that had quit laying. We caught them roosting in guava trees, or they were baited up with scratch feed. When the hens were dressed, every bit of the fat was saved. The carcass was cut at the joints, no cutting or breaking of bones. The same big, black iron chowder pot was used. However, the fire control was most important as the rice had to be soft and tender, but not sticky, each grain separate. (Never stir the pileau pot. It ruins the rice.) Also, the exact amount of black pepper was important. Everyone, young and old, turned to the pot for seconds when this backyard chicken pileau was properly done in the old Palma Sola backyard style.

Believe it or not, only on rare and infrequent occasions was there a jar of good Palma Sola 'shine sneaked around at these cookouts, for those who chose to sample this fiery liquid carried the telltale jar rim mark on the bridge of their nose.

About once each year the ladies of the WCTU, in cooperation with the Sunday school and the public school, would produce an elocution contest. This included everything from a four year old's Bible verse recitation to a teenager's delivery of "The Drunken Organist". However, all of the recitations were supposed to emphasize the evils of drink. The more literate mothers spent much time teaching their children their lines and their ideas of emphasis and delivery in the evenings around the kerosene lamps, while the fathers might be out sneaking a sip of the 'shine or a healthy drink of grapefruit wine.

Attendance at these contests pretty well filled the Palma Sola Church. Always Dr. Parker, a rich Yankee, and her entourage, contributed most of the awards. Although Dr. Parker, according to Palma Sola standards, was wealthy, her degree in homeopathic medicine put her on call in local emergencies. She had an automobile, a yard man, a maid, and a cook, and a twelve room house, formerly the Warner, or Palma Sola, Hotel. She was not a prude, met everyone at their level, and in her generosity arranged for the famous Helen Keller to appear at the Manatee County WCTU Convention. This Dr. Parker could make even a bashful, fourteen year old countrywise cracker boy feel that reciting an anti-booze poem at the WCTU contest was not degrading, and it certainly was an important factor in the improvement of the teenage participant's reading and spelling.

Dr. Parker's medication consisted of some little white pills and sometimes larger white pills. I never heard of her writing a prescription, and her questions regarding the patient's condition were always the same: "How are your bowels?" "What color is your stool?" "Do you see double?" "Are you dizzy?" "Now eat only one meal today and take one of these pills". She always had a supply with her. "Continue the pills morning, noon and night. I am sure that you will feel better tomorrow." "No, there is no charge this time, but see me next week if you are not feeling better."

Dr. Parker later married a Palma Sola widower, and became Mrs. Dr. Bradley. Mr. Bradley had built a five room frame house on the south Loop Road, cultivated a few citrus trees in the poor soil near the tide line in Palma Sola Bay. It was evident that the revenue from this attempt to raise citrus would not support a family. Still, he had a car and was always dressed well, and until her passing, escorted his first wife to the local cultural functions. Otherwise, as was generally practiced, no definite or confirmed details on his reason for leaving the north, settling in rural Palma Sola, and living above cracker standards without visible means of support, was his business, and all wished him well when he closed the little house and moved to the Dr. Parker big house and changed the mailbox sign to Mr. and Dr. C.E. Bradley.

Pursuing an education above the seventh grade level was not simple or easy for Palma Sola youth prior to World War I. Although the county had shelled the road from the corner store into Bradenton, riding a bike with your books and lunch, peddling away from home at 6:45 A.M. rain or shine, for the seven mile jaunt to the new Manatee County High School building was a considerable chore, and you were expected to wear shoes (if you had any). In the cool winter months, making the return trip by dusk or heading into nor'wester at a maximum of three miles per hour, made the price of education high, even with a good bike and family support. Now Bertha Rude's start for school was two and a half miles west of the store, the Rogers' girls two miles, and Honey Warner about one mile. Doris Hampton rode to the school in Bradenton with her dad, who had a car and a business in Bradenton, while the Sikes children, Ruby and Wilbur, and Howard Pettigrew, Clyde Phelps, and John Jennings all started from their homes near the store. The Smiths were usually taken in by Katie, the hard working, ambitious mother, who drove the Ford, and spent every possible moment, early and late, nurturing the family and working in their Lone Palm jelly factory.

Bertha Rude, Ruby Sikes, Howard Pettigrew and Clyde Phelps diligently pursued their education. The Rogers' girls continued on their own to Normal School. Then came the interruption of World War I. The Evans boys were off to an enlistment, Howard Pettigrew and his dad to an assignment in the Tampa shipyards, and Clyde Phelps into the Navy after missing Annapolis by one appointment. The Hall boys, Ruben Stowe, and Bill Sikes all boated out to Ft. Dade to enlist. All were under age, so no enlistment, but being healthy cracker boys, were hired by the quartermaster for manual labor. They worked ten hours each day at hard labor, ate at separate tables at the Army mess hall, slept on cots wherever they cold be set up to avoid the swarms of mosquitos and the heat. Sikes got lucky and was assigned to the dispatch boat that ran errands from Tampa, St. Petersburg, Bradenton and Sarasota.

Around the Palma Sola Loop

The boys' trips to Palma Sola were not looked forward to. First, they had to pay old man Gainey to boat them back and forth, and Palma Sola was dead since all of their peers were away in the service or shipyards, or in some other way connected to the war effort. Even the girls were at Red Cross nurses' training or in war work. Everyone, especially the young, were real flag wavers. On trips to Bradenton for parades, rallies, or home guard meetings, everyone, young and old, stood at attention and saluted or removed hats as the colors passed. Each soul seemed to radiate patriotism. Everyone was ready to shelter and console some enlisted youth, mostly from the North or West, as they tried to find some pleasure in this strange land on their few hours leave from the various cantonments. Home sickness and wonder for the reasons why affected enlisted youths and underage war workers alike. The Palma Sola boys on labor detail at Egmont Key (Ft. Dade) were shocked and scared when the caskets of the flu victims were lined up on the quartermaster's dock. The flu epidemic ran rampant. The only good news, nary a case of flue in Palma Sola, although Cora Davis, a Red Cross nurse and flu victim, was returned to Palma Sola for internment. The young labor boys at the fort, at least those who remained on the job—Ruben Stowe, Ben, and Fred Hall, were on the mainland when the armistice came. They laughed, cried and prayed together, with all the others, and they did not return to the fort, even for their last pay.

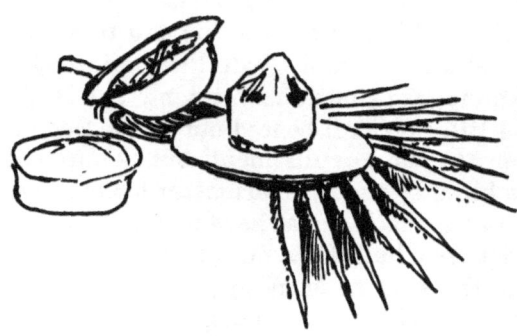

Chapter III

World War I Depression

Post World War I, Palma Sola went through a change. Character, ambition and morals evidenced a before and after change that was impossible to justify and hard to believe. I don't know of a single Palma Sola girl that got "knocked up" before the war. Sure, all of the boys and girls knew what God made the difference between boys and girls for, and don't think that there was no heavy necking during the dating process. Some of the boys and a few girls were considered "fast". With the girls this meant rolled down stockings and loose breast bands, and it was a pity that so many of the firm, beautiful, well formed breasts were mutilated by a tight band that flattened and broke down the girls' beautiful forms. Seldom did the boys, while necking, penetrate the breast band any more than on rare occasions when a finger managed to penetrate the cleavage between the two crushed and desecrated breasts. At moments of passion, conscience, fear, or maybe a peculiar respect for the local girl reversed the opinion that the excited male has no conscience, or, maybe it was just the finality of the girl's "Stop" order. Anyway, the Palma Sola boys went to other communities for their trysts, and were vigilant in their actions against foreign youths invading their territory for less than honorable purposes.

Around the Palma Sola Loop

Palma Sola had a few houses in fair repair for rent, and being rural, they were without electricity or inside plumbing. They, however, did appeal to some Yankees who were looking for a way to plant a wife and children in Florida during the winter, while papa worked his job and, maybe, as a cracker said, kept two home fires burning. This also was an opportunity for the now worldly-wise returned soldiers, sailors, and war workers to offer their services to the northern visitor in her loneliness. Could she resist? Not really, and she could also try a variety, for in the Palma Sola community, changing from purely rural to suburban style after the war, intriques, unhappily, were not honored by confidentiality. The unattached males gladly gave their services and were not reluctant to discuss their intriques while the teenage male neophyte gained an education and had the opportunity to demonstrate what had, heretofore, been only fantasy.

Some of the mothers of the young local studs even contacted the husbands of these winter women. One or two phoned or wrote a letter to check things out. Nothing else happened.

During the first post World War I period a depression, deep and dark, hovered over Palma Sola. There was no work. Soldiers, sailors, marines, and the Coast Guard enlistments were all discharged. All war work was shut down. Even the gathering of wild castor beans for aircraft engine oil was cancelled. The wild guavas in Palma Sola and on Perico Island could, in season, be sold to the jelly factory. A hard ten hour day's work could mean a couple of dollars, if you could fight off the redbugs and mosquitos, and dodge the rattlesnakes. Mullet were 2 cents per pound, if delivered to the fish house in prime condition. Grouper was 4 cents in the round, and the rare road or field job, 7:00 A.M. to 5:00 P.M., paid $1.50 if it did not rain. There were no food stamps, no relief or welfare, but no one starved, and folks either became Holy Rollers or scoundrels. There seemed to be no in-between. The girls played around, moonshining became rampant. Whiskey running was considered necessary for the economy. Bacardi rum dropped to $4.00 per gallon retail, wickerbound jug and all, and the rum was easily picked up direct from Cuban boats close to our shore. But who had $4.00?

World War I Depression

Palma Sola had its post-war exodus. There was no reason for anybody to stay in Palma Sola who wanted to work for a living and have shoes with socks, be able to sleep in a house with electric lights and a water closet, maybe some day have a car, and even be able to send a dollar or two home to help out the old folks. The girls who had gone to school took off for nurses' training, or if it could be arranged, a summer session at Tallahassee Florida Normal, where a tenth grade high school girl could earn a teacher's certificate in one summer session and have a chance to have a job teaching at $45 per month in a backwoods rural school. Otherwise, employment was spotty, seasonal, and with poor pay. Canning factories or packing house jobs still meant six months of starvation.

The boys could try to make groceries if they could finance a skipjack, a poling oar and three hundred yards of gill net, then work hard for little more than starvation wages. Dredge boats and following the sea offered some few tramp-type jobs. Private yachting was only good for six months each year. Maybe the circus. If you landed a job with Ringling you were "in", if you kept your nose clean and were observed by the family. A few of the boys from Palma Sola made good with the circus. Some became "in and outers"—they would be away for a period and then return. They always seemed to have a few dollars to sustain them, wore reasonably good clothes and maybe made a temporary hook-up with moonshiners, bootleggers or whiskey runners.

Only two of the pre-war farmers returned to the soil to slave eight months a year in a truck patch, cut out a car of celery, or crate up a car or so of peppers or tomatoes, if lucky, pay off the fertilizer house, dress up and take off for an Ybor City brothel for two or three week-ends. Then start the same routine all over again. Small truck farming was not for the family man.

Around the Palma Sola Loop

Chapter IV

Off and On
The Palma Sola Loop Road

Old Palma Sola was not devoid of stable family structures. Starting south from Hop's store and following the Palma Sola Loop Road, south-west-north-east, and south to the point of beginning, you passed homes or crossed the entry road ruts to all of the regular old Palma Sola residences, not one of which had inside plumbing or electricity. On this route you might encounter a few drifters or, near a dilapidated shack, some unemployed field hands, and possibly, some unidentified beachcombers. No questions asked.

As we travel around the Loop Road from the store, first we pass the three room house of Aunt Nancy Hopper, where she lived with her daughter and son. Aunt Nancy was a tall, slim widow woman who would do housework or laundry. She came to Palma Sola after the loss of her husband because her sister, Aunt Dora, was married to Captain Frank Pillsbury. More about Frank Pillsbury later. Aunt Nancy was known to visit Snead's Island for the Adventist church service, courtesy of Captain Ed Pillsbury, who met her at the dock in his light tending boat "Pilgrim". Although Captain Ed had a large house and a large family on Snead's Island, on the return of Aunt Nancy to the Palma Sola side the Pilgrim was moored at a less conspicuous place so that it would not be bothered, while Capt. Ed took Aunt Nancy home and they enjoyed a review of the church services while laying in the crisp spruce pine needles on the white sand mound near Aunt Nancy's back door.

Around the Palma Sola Loop

After the death of Capt. Ed's first wife, Aunt Nancy was employed as his housekeeper. Unfortunately, the church directed that Capt. Ed should marry a semi-invalid church widow. However, Aunt Nancy stayed on as the hardworking housekeeper for the large family until her daughter, Laura, married Asa Pillsbury III, Capt. Ed's son, after which Aunt Nancy moved in with them for a more leisurely life.

The next home down the road was a one room cabin occupied by one Mr. Hoag, a bachelor, probably in his late sixties, and rumored to be a retired Yankee school teacher, and a loner. Always in a wool suit, slow of gait, short and stocky, he responded very cordially to all greetings, and spent one evening a week in the Hall's attic where Ben and Fred Hall, Ruben and Alonza Stowe were given a one hour class in rapid calculations, spelling, and penmanship, for a fee of 25 cents per week per student, usually on credit.

At the southeast corner of the Loop Road there was a small culvert under the road and a large slew leading into Warner's west bayou. At the bayou end of the culvert where the slew widened was a good sized gator wallow. The Hall boys made a few dollars selling foot long baby gators for 25 cents each. Ben also received a severely injured finger joint when snapped by a little three foot gator. Meandering away from this corner were two sand ruts passing Mr. Allion's tangerine grove and ending in the woods some one-half mile south in the yard of Uncle Bill and Aunt Ellen Long, the only colored folks in Palma Sola. Bill was a foreman at Crocker's celery farm and Aunt Ellen would do housework or help with canning and butchering. There was no friction between white and black here. Bill and Ellen kept to themselves and lived back in the woods. Bill was the best bird-dog trainer and quail shot in the county. In the season he shot so many quail that they pickled them down in five gallon crocks.

Fronting 1320 feet on the south side of the south Loop Road was the Brook's farm, share cropped by Jay Hall supported by his wife Lillie. There were ten acres of grove and five acres of truck land, a long scuppernong arbor and some Japanese persimmon trees. The large frame house, sort of like a salt box design, was rather a nice house in those days, with a closed-in sleeping porch on the east side and large covered porches on the rear and west. The boys slept in the unfinished attic close to the roof, where the temperature stayed in the 90s eight months of the year. The girls, Papa Jay and Mother Lillie had regular spring and mattress beds downstairs, while the boys had "corn shuck mattresses" that consisted of the standard gray and white striped ticking made into an envelope and stuffed with dried corn shucks, which were not only noisy, but body movement would cause a separation of the corn shucks, leaving you laying in or covered with only two thin layers of bed ticking.

Rose, the oldest daughter, finished high school in Bradenton and went on to nurses' training. Ben and Fred, the youthful boys, were home only at intervals, as Papa Jay was pretty tough, and demanded labor or board money. Jay Jr. and Sheila May, the two younger children, were the apple of Papa's eye and could do no wrong.

This Hall family migrated to Palma Sola from Bisbee, Arizona, via Bradenton. Papa Jay had a prosperous barber shop, bath house and restaurant in Arizona, which he sold, along with a modest mountainside bungalow home when the territory of Arizona gained statehood. He did not like Arizona state laws and regulations. He landed in Florida with his lifetime earnings strapped to his belly in a money belt.

A quick venture in barber shopping in Bradenton did not work out. Shaves at 15 cents, haircuts at a quarter, and no baths hardly compared with the busy Arizona fifty cent shaves, dollar haircuts, with a 30 minute hot water tub bath at $2.50, plus the factor that Papa Jay had developed a stubborn attitude. He just did not operate on a basis that would cause anyone to lend a helping hand. This was especially true after he started farming, and it took just two seasons for all of his capital to be dissipated, and he joined the ranks of the stoney broke sharecroppers. Mother Hall was the opposite: a lovable, God-fearing, educated lady from the old Pennsylvania Penn family, loved by all, a fine mother and homemaker, with never a cross word to Papa Jay in spite of his rough treatment of the older boys.

Ben and Fred, at the ages of 16 and 14, were seldom seen around the Hall home. Dredge boats, private yachts, packing houses in Florida and a trip to the midwestern harvest fields and stone quarries kept them busy. The boys worked hard for a living, and the stint as laborers at Ft. Dade during World War I toughened them up for meeting the difficult times ahead. Rose, the oldest daughter, returned from a war nurse assignment with a husband and a promise of the Hall's first grandchild. Clarence Howard Andress appeared in due time. Ben made out dragging a chain for a surveyor and later, by self education, became a licensed civil engineer, married a beautiful little Cracker girl and raised four successful children. Fred worked his way, or part way, through Tampa Business College; he got thrown out when his two jobs failed to provide the $5.00 a week for board, room and laundry, plus tuition. He followed packing house jobs, private yachting and auto sales until he obtained his real estate license and notary public appointment.

The two youngest Hall children, Jay Jr. and Sheila Mae, remained at home until the mid 20's. Sheila, after a stint as a nurse with Ringling Brothers Circus, married well and frequently. Jay Jr. took a job assignment in Pittsburg, Pennsylvania where he married and started his family. However, the Cracker in him prevailed; he returned to Florida and continued the family process—four nice kids before his demise.

Mr. Brooks sold the farm place to a Mr. Ferguson from Chicago, so the Halls moved to the old Simpson orphanage house in Pine Hurst. Mr. Ferguson started to boil off the corn for his own consumption, which was no small amount. Unfortunately his home-made still exploded, and the nice old house burned to the ground.

On up the south Loop Road on the next forty was the home of Bert Warner, a board and batten two story house where Bert, his wife Elsie, daughter Marian, and two sons, Curtis and Joe, lived. Now Bert was the son of Grandma Warner, who had at one time owned hundreds of acres from Warner's Bayou to Tampa Bay, including Shaw's Point and the giant shell mound, now completely excavated. The property is now known as DeSoto Landing. Although Bert could have also had the advantage of the Warner prestige and wealth, he chose to claim 80 acres along the south Loop Road, which at one point touched Palma Sola Bay. Rumor had it that Bert couldn't be bothered with courting so he advertised for a bride. Elsie from Indiana answered and in a few months showed up in Florida and immediately married Bert. Elsie was no "throwed out" girl, but an educated young lady of moderate circumstances. A few months after she arrived and married Bert the members of her church in Indiana, as news from Elsie was sparse, sent a delegation to Palma Sola to check up and were delighted with what they found. Elsie made a statement at a WCTU meeting shortly after the birth of her youngest son, Joe, when some of the good ladies attempted to console her for the birthing pains encountered, and were emphatically told by Elsie that she would rather have a baby than have a tooth pulled. This statement, through the party lines, store and Post Office gossip, rapidly covered the entire area, and, needless to say, not without exaggeration.

Bert, an introvert, was an excellent craftsman, built boats, did fine carpentry, and made most of the coffins for those who passed away in Palma Sola. Bert's tools, gardens and trees, and always a milk cow or two, kept him busy. Elsie did her duty with the WCTU, seldom attended church services, and kept a good home. Marian, usually called Honey, was the oldest child. She rode her bike the seven miles each way to Manatee County High School, and on Sunday pedalled up to Warner's East Bayou. From her grandmother Warner's house there, she went by horse and buggy to morning services at the Episcopal Church in Fogartyville; after dinner at Grandma's she bicycled back home. After finishing high school she worked in real estate problems but found time to marry and become active in civic affairs. I am not sure if Curtis, the oldest boy, finished high school, but there is no doubt about his ability to make a dollar and keep it. Boiling off a little corn may have appealed to him at intervals. Joe, the youngest, loved his cows, tended and milked them, and developed a small milk route in Palma Sola and Cortez. Joe later became a prominent Manatee County cattleman.

Directly across the Loop Road from the Bert Warner home Mr. Potter, a young gentleman from New England, purchased ten acres of good hammock land, a two story shell of a house, a small barn and an excellent six inch artesian well. After a short period of batching, Mr. Potter took off to return some three months later with a very attractive young wife. He hired a couple of the local teenage boys for the farm chores, while he and his new bride entertained them, and also some of the

Around the Palma Sola Loop

peeking neighbors, with their antics and games, especially the trip to the well where the high, two inch wagon barrel filling pipe created a twenty gallon a minute cool sulpher water shower. The honeymoon was short lived. The Potters took off and the property was sold to a Mr. B.W. Vaughn, a successful and well financed Missouri farmer who later expanded the Potter plot and obtained the deserted, overgrown Durant tract.

Meandering south from the Bert Warner corner a woods road passed the Hampton house where Harry Hampton, an artist, sign painter and decorator, moved his family into a six room bungalow on five acres of mediocre pine and scrub land in 1916. Doris, the oldest child, a charming young lady, and Willis and Chester, the two boys, became part of Palma Sola social life. However, the children went to school in Bradenton, where Harry had his shop, and was the only artist certified to apply gold leaf to window glass in the area south of Tampa. Incidentally, Willis Hampton married Janet Barney, the favorite granddaughter of Mrs. Wilburton Warner (Grandma Warner), who was the real matriarch of old Palma Sola.

The sand ruts parted at the Hamptons. One set went to the west to Captain Adams homestead, where the Captain, his wife, and their adopted son, Johnny and his wife, Tressie, the eldest daughter of Uncle Jim Felts, of Uncle Jim's first litter, lived on Palma Sola Bay. The south road fork wandered off through the woods, forded Palma Sola Creek, and on to Cortez. This was an alternate route for the mailman on his Palma Sola/Cortez mail delivery.

The Adams family was the only resident on the north east shore of Palma Sola Bay. Harry Tallent had a small grove on a marshy section of the bay shore about a mile south of the Adams near Palma Sola Creek. Grandpa Pillsbury's and George Stafford's were the only bay front homes on the south shore. All the rest of the Palma Sola Bay shore line was uninhabited except for a fish camp and moonshiner's shack and landing near the bay channel into Sarasota Sound.

Most of the shore line of this shallow water mossy bottom bay was scrub palmetto or mangrove marsh right down to the high tide line. The beach, if any, was generally muddy or dirty looking sand.

Off and On The Palma Sola Loop Road

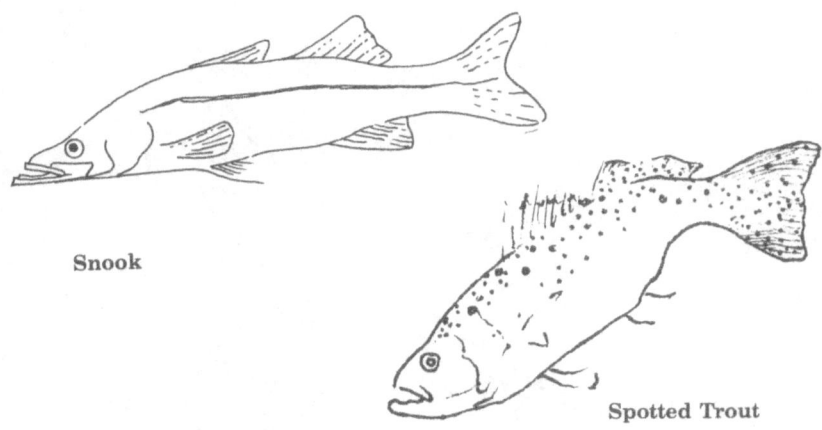

Snook

Spotted Trout

Palma Sola Bay was not inviting to the commercial fisherman, although the shallow mossy bottom areas teemed with speckled trout, which meant success for the hook and line fisherman. Johnny Adams made out fairly well as a trout fisherman, and poled his 14-foot cypress skiff to the Cortez fish house, and in the best of times received 4 cents a pound for his catch.

Saw fish of all sizes, 14 inches to 14 feet, ganged up, multiplied, and played havoc with the net fishermen in Palma Sola Bay. Should the fisherman surround one or more of these monsters while striking for mullet or bottom fish, the big saw simply tore up the net, wound up in it and thrashed around, tearing at the net until nothing was left to salvage but the cork and lead line, which meant many hours of hard, dirty labor.

Most any kid in Palma Sola would sell you a 6 or 8 inch saw for a quarter, or a 4-foot specimen for 4 dollars. Saw fish harvesting was not considered a profitable occupation.

The bay did have its favorable characteristics. Much of the bottom was literally paved with giant Cohog clams. Snook were easily caught or gigged, but in those days snook were scrap fish and not fit for the table, and they were the prime enemy of the mullet fishermen, as one 6 pound snook could and would make a man-sized hole in the gill net.

Around the Palma Sola Loop

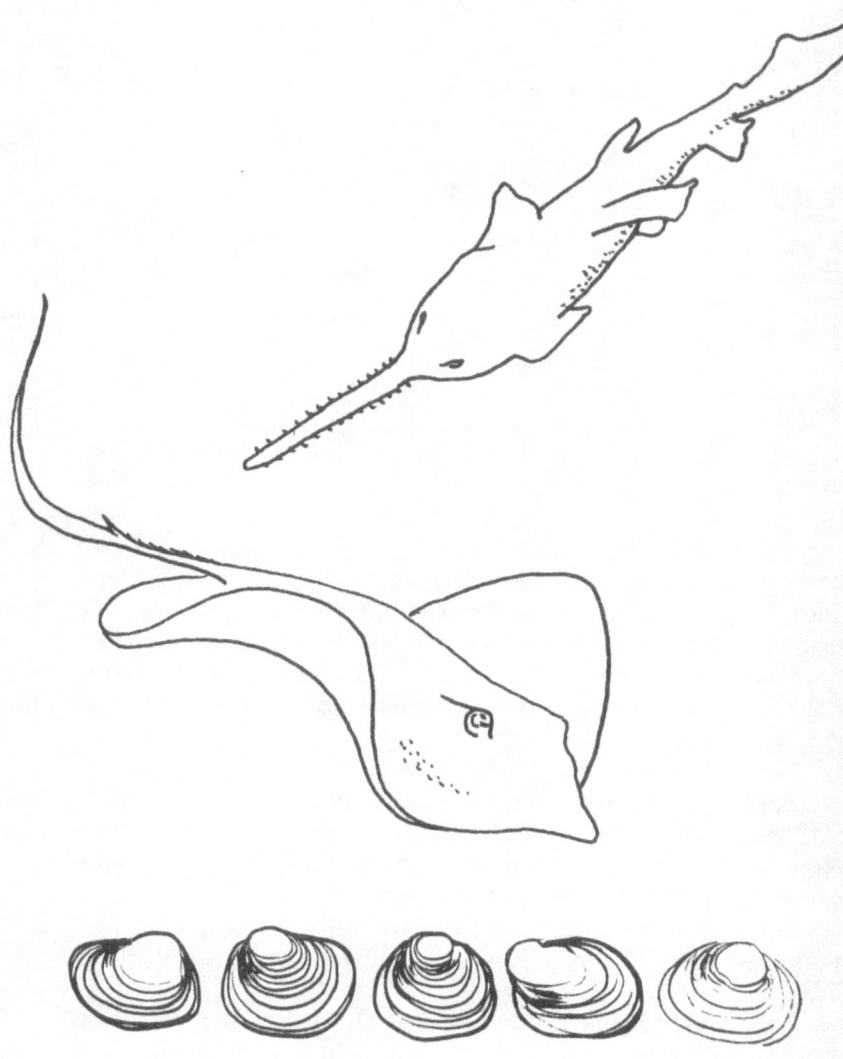

Maybe the fact that Palma Sola Bay had more sting rays per square foot than any other nearby water was the reason so many and such large saw fish were around. The fishermen said the saws lived on sting rays and clams.

Off and On The Palma Sola Loop Road

On Captain Adams' home place a large artesian well was drilled, and believe it or not, the well produced soft sweet water. This well later became the source of "Shorelands" brand bottled water.

Off in the jungle north of the south Loop Road, about 1500 feet west of Bert Warner's, was the ruins of the old Durant house, built around the turn of the century, a reasonably good four room cottage, but built on the ground in a low muck land spot where water covered the floor each rainy season and the road in became difficult even for the mule and wagon. Anyway, Mrs. Durant, a cousin of Fred Sikes, just shut the door one day and moved out. Within a few months the deserted place was covered with tropical vines and brush and between the heavy, tropical vegetation, termites, snakes, racoons, possums and lizards, the house collapsed over the organ, all of the furniture, lamps, dishes and clothes. We kids cut a trail into the site with machetes some years after the place was deserted and found little to salvage.

On the west side of the Durant track on the north side of the road were a few acres of low muck land, also a dilapidated cement building. Col. Snead, a gentleman bachelor, well educated and somewhat of a loner, planted cane in the muck land, shored up the old building, built himself a syrup evaporator pan. He was smart and talented when it came to making things work. For two seasons many gallons of good cane syrup were produced from the Colonel's cane patch and the Christian Endeavor had several "sugar pills" as Col. Snead's guests. A "sugar pill" is a party where a certain amount of cane syrup is boiled down to a very thick consistency. Then, as it cools, it is pulled like taffy, into a delicious cane flavored tan colored taffy candy. The Colonel got tired of the syrup project, moved back to his room at the store, where he bached, played his fiddle, occasionally accommodated a selected widow or lonesome lady. The cane patch became a jungle and the Colonel finally ended up as a cancer victim.

The next house on the road was a one room shack on a sand hill 200 feet off the road. Here Sol Switzer lived with his son, Austin "Bud", and daughter Julia. How they existed is a mystery. Sol Switzer was the son of Captain Austin Switzer, who sailed a trading schooner from the Florida west coast to

Around the Palma Sola Loop

Havana, Cuba. His cargo mostly salt fish, was in high demand in Cuba. Capt. Austin Switzer, while docked in Havana, became acquainted with the DeNoda family, who were in route from the Canary Islands to Florida, where they planned to homestead land on the Gulf or Tampa Bay. Capt. Austin's description of Palma Sola so impressed the DeNodas that they were anxious to proceed. They sold their large sailboat and bought a small one suitable for the Florida coast and the Palma Sola area. Capt. Austin Switzer's son, Sol, was then assigned the task of piloting the new boat, with the DeNoda family, to Palma Sola, with a stopover at Panther Key. Sol had an eye for the DeNoda daughter, whom he later married, and much later, lived in the old DeNoda house on the south Loop Road. Rumors were circulated as to their circumstances, none very enlightening or pleasant. However, the family lived in the old DeNoda house near Palma Sola Bay until Mrs. Sol Switzer died, reportedly of malnutrition. There were four children, three girls and one boy. The two older girls, according to rumor, were made wards of the county. Sol and the two youngest children, Bud and Julia, moved to the one room shack just east of the church, cemetery and school property.

The grade school Palma Sola girls walking the shell ruts to school were prone to, thumb in ears, tongue waggle at the Switzer girl, who would be peeking around the corner at them. The children cruelly reported Julia as half witted owing to incest, and refused her any contact with her peers. Had Palma Sola not been so set in ways of "don't mess in somebody else's affair", maybe the fate of the last remnant of the Switzer family would have been different.

Along in this same area a foot path moved off northward through the brush where the widow Stowe lived in a ramshackled, falling down, four room house with her family, Alonza, Ruben and Mary. The eldest daughter, Anna, had married Graton Felts. They lived in the tenant house on the Stafford place. Alonzo Stowe was a big, handsome, young man, but, unfortunately, was epileptic, thus was mostly unemployed. He did land a job as a deck hand on Capt. Bishop's motor ship, The Peerless, a small freight boat operating from Tampa to Cortez, Westview and Sarasota. While the Peerless was moored at the Sarasota freight docks, Alonzo had a sei-

Off and On The Palma Sola Loop Road

zure, fell over board and was drowned. After a Ft. Dade labor stint, Ruben worked for an affluent gentleman as handyman and chauffer. This man treated Ruben as a son, later paid his tuition, board and room while attending barber college. Mary, the youngest, had a bad leg from polio. She and Mother Stowe left Palma Sola shortly after the Armistice and moved in with relatives in the Charlotte County backwoods.

Palma Sola Church

On down the south Loop Road, up a little grade, probably a six foot rise in elevation, was the location of the school house, church and cemetery. The beautiful little Palma Sola Church was built of cement block, cast at the location by the loving hands of the congregation. The construction supervised by Jim Felts and Deacon Rogers. Over the entrance way was a steeple,

Around the Palma Sola Loop

but no bell. The doors, window sills and frames, and the floor were of long leaf pine, original growth, square edge, knot free, and sound. The attractive pews were of the same material, handcrafted by local artisans.

Deacon Rogers, the Sunday school superintendent, always wore a jacket, a celluloid collar with no tie—a gold collar button was quite obvious. The Deacon made the opening and closing prayers with his eyes wide open and led the singing of the hymns. The hymns I will always remember and revere: beautiful old Protestant songs sung with enthusiasm, the lyrics in some way sinking in, to be hummed and considered during the week while tending crops or awaiting the haul of a gill net or seine.

On the south side of the road was the Stafford property. Grandpa Pillsbury had sold ten acres to George Stafford, a Yankee of some affluence. He built a nice, two story house, barn and tenant house of three rooms. The big house faced the bay, with a four foot wide, two hundred fifty foot dock with a boat house at the deep water end. A few fruit trees and some ornamentals were planted and the entire ten acres was grubbed and fenced. Brush was always kept cut down so there were no wild jungles or tall grasses anywhere.

George was a pleasant, outgoing man who liked his little nip, both real red liquor and white shine, and it was most always evident that one or the other was contributing to his pleasures. Mrs. Stafford was no snob, but was not active in church or WCTU. She was always happy and ready with the dollar to help out.

Next to the Stafford home was Grandpa Pillsbury's homestead, a large, two story house, facing Palma Sola Bay on relatively small acreage, considering that Grandpa had once owned hundreds of acres on Palma Sola Bay extending over halfway north to Tampa Bay on both sides of the Loop Road. His dock was the only one on the north side of Palma Sola Bay until the Staffords came along, and was still considered public property by fishermen and those who still used boats for transportation. This dock was handy to church, cemetery, and school, and the water route was much shorter than roaming through the wood's road around the south and east end of Palma Sola Bay.

Off and On The Palma Sola Loop Road

Pillsbury house

Grandpa Pillsbury enjoyed the visits of all of his close friends and kin. Grandpa was Asa N. Pillsbury, Sr. His children, Asa N, Jr., Capt. Ed, Mr. Frank and Mamie, and his youngest son William. All of the children remained in the Palma Sola area, excepting William, who thought he was imposed upon, ran away and went to sea. He then enlisted in the Navy and died a natural death in the Naval hospital in Brooklyn, New York, at the start of World War I. Capt. Ed owned and operated Pillsbury's Boat Ways on Snead's Island, was a devout Seventh Day Adventist and a United States contract light tender for Tampa Bay and the Manatee River. Mamie married Hal Phelps, who became one of Palma Sola's most prominent citizens. More about Asa Jr. and Frank as we continue around the Loop Road.

Across the road, just west of the church, on a small plot, was the home of Deacon Rogers. His house of cement block cast by the Deacon and his two sons was never completely finished inside. The family consisted of the Deacon and his wife, Mary, two boys Carlyle and Douglas, four girls Agnes, Lena, Nettie and Myrtle, in that order. A hard working, God fearing family. Douglas never came back to live in Palma Sola after World War I. He visited once with his British war bride.

Around the Palma Sola Loop

Carlyle worked as a carpenter and cabinet maker and married a local girl, one Carry Harvey, daughter of a squatter family living in old Pinehurst. Carry made Carlyle a devoted partner. Agnes worked as a department head in Woolworths in Tampa until she was married. Lena married Clyde Phelps and taught school on Anna Maria Island for many years. Nettie became a government girl in Washington, D.C., returned to Florida as an old maid to retire, while Myrtle made a real name for herself in the Manatee County School system, married Red Rhoden, raised her family and took care of the Deacon in his final years after he became blind. Lena and Myrtle were the prime movers in religious activities in Palma Sola. Myrtle played the wheezy, old, foot treadle organ for church, Sunday school and Christian Endeavor, with Lena singing solos, usually slightly off key. Myrtle pumped out the music on the old organ with such difficulty that she appeared to be pumping a bicycle up a steep grade against a headwind. Myrtle, when a child, was struck on the heel by a rattlesnake, which she stepped on while trotting to the privy. No lasting bad effects.

There was no scandal in the Rogers Family, maybe a little rumor about the Deacon's calls at the Toland house on Perico Island Road. I am sure the stopover there was only to water his mule, Tipparary.

Across the road and further west was the Bradly house, a small bungalow facing the road in a small citrus grove. The property ran south to Palma Sola Bay. This area was not used as it was low and marshy, not even covered with mangrove, no channel from the bay, no dock or boat landing. The Bradlys were not salt water oriented. Their one daughter, Cecil, an artist was not a snob, but spent little time with the local society. Mr. Bradly, after the loss of his wife, married Dr. Parker, the eminent owner of the old Warner Hotel on Warner's Point. Adjoining the old Bradly place on the west, set back from the road, was a small four room frame house occupied by Charlie Pettigrew. Although Charlie's brothers, John J. and Ed., were both prominent in Palma Sola, Charlie was seldom seen around, nor did his family participate in any activities.

A half mile or so of rutted roadway continued west with no permanent residents on either side. Frank "Jelly Factory" Smith had ten acres of guavas on the south side and Ross Felts

Off and On The Palma Sola Loop Road

had a five acre sharecrop truck patch on the north side. This plot was later known as the Tubby Evans Farm.

At the southwest corner of the Loop Road two trails led off through the wilderness, one due west to Perico Bayou sandflats where, at the tide line, was a two room shack, owned by Mr. E.P. Moore, and was usually occupied by squatters. In one case, the senior male of the squatter family, in the Moore shack, sickened and died. The news spread. Lillie Hall and Agnes Rogers responded and were horrified to find that for some cult reasons none of the family would go into the house where the corpse lay. As usual, Bert Warner and Jim Felts built the box. The good ladies of the WCTU lined the box, dressed the corpse, and Deacon Rogers' wagon picked up the coffin and transported it to the Palma Sola cemetery, where the remains received a Christian burial.

The Perico Bayou sand flats were an unusual phenomenon, the Bayou not normally navigable, had a few hip-deep holes with ankle-deep trickles connecting them except at storm high tides. The sand flats were table top smooth, with only a slight scattering of dwarf mangrove or tuft grass. This area extended from Palma Sola Bay to Tampa Bay, and was from a few hundred feet to a mile wide.

Besides the thousands of sea birds that frequented the flats, there were millions of fiddler crabs. To see these fiddlers wave their big claw in unison with all the others was an unbelievable sight. Fiddler crabs are excellent sheephead and redfish bait. We kids would find an area where they were thick, then start running in a 20 or 30 foot circle, gradually closing in until the crabs were a foot deep, to be scooped up by the bucketfull for bait and chicken feed.

Male fiddler crabs have one large fighting claw, and one very small feeder claw. The large fighting claw is maneuvered like a violin player's bow, and in unison with the hundreds of other male crabs in the area. The females are smaller, and have two very small feeder claws. Usually two varieties cohabit—the larger ones pink and white colored, and the smaller variety a dull brown.

Around the Palma Sola Loop

Among the birds that frequented the flats were gannets (wood ibis), curlew, plover and snipes, and a few wild ducks in the adjacent ponds—all then considered edible game birds—and many ended up on the tables of the natives.

The other trail meandered southwest, past the Toland house. Mr. Toland was a piano tuner, working out of a Bradenton piano store (Hullingers). Mrs. Toland was, it seems, absent from the home for days at a time. This meant that Dorothy, the oldest daughter, barely a teen-ager, ran the ranch much of the time, as the other Toland child, a younger girl, was less than competent. This put a heavy responsibility on Dorothy. This same road went past the George Breese sparsely worked truck patch as it meandered off to the first narrow plank fording bridge across the Perico Bayou slosh channel. Deacon Rogers did some custom mule power work for George Breese, so it was handy for him to water his mule, Tipparary, at the Tolands, when he could visit with Mrs. Toland and check up on their general condition.

Off and On The Palma Sola Loop Road

Turn the corner north and the Jim Felts property was on the west side. Uncle Jim Felts originated in Georgia with his first family, then moved to St. Augustine, where the world famous Flagler Hotel was being built. He worked there as a boss carpenter. Word of the even larger, more elaborate Tampa Bay Hotel being constructed in Tampa appealed to Jim Felts, so he took off for Tampa and was taken on by Mr. H.B. Plant as boss carpenter and cabinet maker. He was personally in charge of the carpenter work in the famous hostelry. From there he came to Manatee County with his large family. His first stop was in Cortez, where he built some of the still-standing homes that house the old Cortez fishing families. He then settled on a large acreage of high land, not counting the sand flats of Perico Bayou that met this high land on the west. Uncle Jim's first family of six children all came to Palma Sola with him. After losing his first wife he married Idell Prince and continued the family process by producing a second litter of nine children.*

Jim Felts was a hard working, talented, temperate man, who knew how to do for himself and live off the land. He brought in many semitropical fruits and vegetables to feed the dozens who were around his table. They ate well, both in volume and quality, as well as aroma and delectable taste. The nami, roasted and served with garlic butter, the pickled choyote, cornbread with homemade cane syrup, guava paste, sweet potato pudding, plus home butchered pork and chicken, plus game from the woods and salt ponds, fed all of the young ones from Palma Sola who liked to be around the table at meal time, and even between meals. There was always a tasty meal or pick up, fruits, honey, vegetables or game.

All of the Felt's children were talented. Not a single lazy or snobbish one in the lot, and there was a wide age range, from Graten at 40 to Princella at 1. On the trips to the store a Ford Chassis with a box over the gas tank for the driver's seat provided transportation. A cross plank platform on the truck rails supported cargo and kids, even on the very infrequent trips to Tampa, where Uncle Jim always had arrangements for some special tools, seeds or plants, to expand the production of his live-off-the-land accomplishments.

*See Epilogue

Around the Palma Sola Loop

For some time Jim Felts principle money crop was cane syrup. His particular species of ribbon cane was some 8 foot to the bud, 2 inches in diameter and heavy in syrup producing juice. However, the development of his bee gums was growing and continued to multiply until the cane syrup project was abandoned in favor of honey production.

On one of these Tampa trips a large bunch of ripe bananas was purchased from the vendor at the boat docks, which adjoined the road to the city from the south. These streetside vendors sold the over-ripe Honduran bananas at 50 cents per stock, or 5 cents for a large hand. The Felt's children on the truck were feasting on these ripe bananas as the truck proceeded homeward to Palma Sola. At the Manatee County line a Mediterranean fruit fly quarantine had been set up. When the inspector told Uncle Jim that he could not take the fruit into Manatee County he pulled the truck well of the road and said "kids, eat up, we can't waste ripe bananas".

Across the road from the Felt's house was the Rude place, a nice looking, well kept bungalow, no grove, a combination barn and garage and a small truck farm. Mr. Rude was a traveling salesman, covering all of the eastern United States, so he paid only infrequent visits to the Rude home. Mrs. Rude, a very attractive lady ran the ranch, did little, if any, money crop farming, and took care of Bertha, Mr. Rude's daughter by a former marriage. Bertha was a beautiful girl, rather shy. She rode her bike from the west Loop Road to Manatee High, some nine miles, over bad road. She finished high school. Bertha was not too popular a date for the Christian Endeavor, or church activities, as the walk to pick her up and return her home after the activities could add up to six miles, and Bertha's religion, plus a strict moral code, prohibited any heavy necking stopovers enroute.

Further down, the west end Loop Road was unsettled, except for a ten acre corner where John Pettigrew, the well driller, had started a truck patch and small nursery, worked mostly by Howard, his eldest son. But more about the John Pettigrews later, as they lived back on the dock road off the northeast corner of the loop.

Off and On The Palma Sola Loop Road

From the west end of the north side Loop Road, running for about one mile east, several sand rut wagon trails led off through the scrub to the north. The westernmost and least traveled led to Seven Pines Point, and Old Smith Bayou on the south shore of Tampa Bay where the ruins of an old board and batten two room shack haunted an overgrown patch of guava and scrub. The area contained the remnants of many a camp fire as Seven Pines Point was rich grounds for clams, stone crabs and scallops in season.

All along this old rutted road, with washed out spots and some overgrown areas, was heavy evidence of camp-out, hideout, beachcombing or picnicking. Palm stumps dotted the area where swamp cabbage (Palm hearts) had been chopped out and all about dead coals, clam, oyster and other shells, both ancient and recent remained.

The Seven Pines Point shallow water expanse extended from Tampa Bay into Sarasota sound in the area of Smith's Bayou, and on these mossy bottom flats there occurred a yearly phenomenon as thousands of sting rays concentrated, many of them in the hundred pound size or over. The surface of the water would dance like schools of roe mullet bunching. It was the sting rays mating season and when a Cortez fishing crew in the moonlight, or even daylight, mistook the congregated sting rays for mullet and made a strike, they were confronted with the problem of freeing their nets from the hundreds of rays of all sizes.

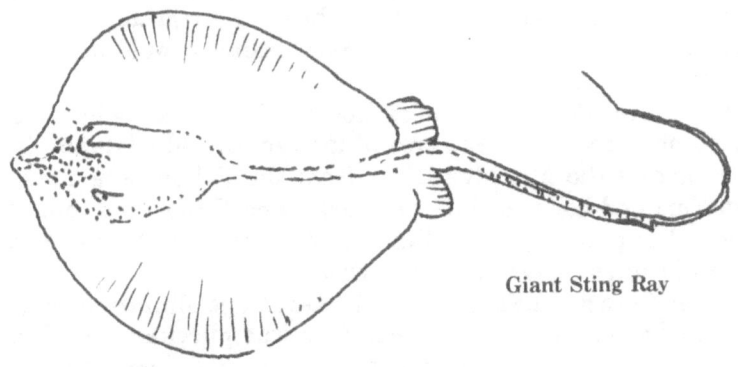

Giant Sting Ray

Around the Palma Sola Loop

The next set of ruts led off northward to the property of Asa N. Pillsbury, Jr., generally known as Uncle Asa. This talented and somewhat opinionated gentleman had followed marine activity all of his life. He had been master or first mate on both sail and motor vessels, working the Florida coast and nearby islands. He had earned a reputation as a boat builder, and, with his brother, Frank, conducted a boat building and boat repair ways in a large, two-story, wooden building at the foot of the Palma Sola Dock. Asa also built a small house back of the boat shop. This small house was designed similar to a schooner cabin or deck house, suitable for Uncle Asa's bachelor quarters, but not intended to accommodate a family. Therefore, after his marriage to a widow with two children, the second floor of the boat shop and the small house were used as family living quarters until the boat shop, the house and the land were sold to Mr. B.M. Allion to be converted into a general store.

After the sale of the boat shop and his marriage to the widow from New Orleans, one Cora Earl, nee Peitavent, Asa built a shelter shack for his family, that is wife Cora, and children, Carlos and Elinor, on Passage Key, a sand spit void of any permanent vegetation, but the resting place and nesting haven for literally thousands of sea birds. Cora was a fanatic bird watcher. However, as Passage Key had been designated a wildlife refuge, Uncle Asa was ordered to vacate his squatter shelter. He and family camped out on Egmont Key for a short period before moving to the bay front twenty acre plot he had bought from Pearson Nickols, where he built a two story frame house between a large pre-Columbian Indian mound and the high tide line of Tampa Bay.

Capt. Jim Peitavent, the father of Uncle Asa's wife, had settled on three hundred acres of land on Snead's Island, directly across the Manatee River from the Palma Sola Dock. Cora Earl and her two children, Carlos and Elinor, had moved in with her parents, Capt. Jim and Mara Peitavent, after the death of Cora's husband in New Orleans.

After Cora's marriage to Uncle Asa, Capt. Jim decided to sell the Snead's Island acreage. This was purchased by Mr. Peter Marine, a well to do candy manufacturer from Chicago. A sales contract was agreed upon, duly signed, sealed and re-

Off and On The Palma Sola Loop Road

corded. When the date for closing arrived, Capt. Jim decided that he did not want to sell, and offered Peter Marine his deposit money back, plus profit. No sale! Mr. Marine wanted the property. Whereupon Capt. Jim demanded payment in gold coin or no sale. The court upheld the gold demand and allowed Mr. Marine thirty days extension to come up with the gold coin. Whereupon Mr. Marine took off for Chicago and returned three weeks later loaded down with the gold. A settlement date and place were established. At this meeting Capt. Jim again pleaded for Mr. Marine to call the deal off, receive his money back, with a profit, which again was refused. Capt. Jim then accepted the gold coin, stepped directly in front of Mr. Marine and spat in his face as he departed.

After Uncle Asa's wife, Cora, and the teenage children, Carlos and Elinor, were settled in their permanent home on Tampa Bay, Uncle Asa planted the whole area, except the big Indian mound and the small pond adjacent to the mound, in hybrid mangos.

Asa received slight, if any help from Carlos; although he was a big husky youth, never did his hands develop callouses. Reading and dreaming were his thing. He attended the Palma Sola school intermittently, a few days at a time walking the woods path the two and one-half miles to the school then being absent weeks at a time. When asked to recite on his assigned subjects, he was always A+, almost professional. Elinor wrote poetry and read while not accompanying her mother on birding expeditions. However, if you were to encounter them while beachcombing, they simply disappeared into the jungle.

Maybe once a year Cora would accompany Asa to the post office or into town to sign papers. Otherwise she had no contact with the outside world.

Carlos and Elinor did nave one contact with their peers, as each summer King Wiggins, a Manatee merchant and businessman, took his family to an isolated cottage on Tampa Bay some five hundred feet up the beach from Uncle Asa's place. Carlos and Elinor both became enamored and had platonic affairs with the Wiggins children in the summer time. Rumor had it that Elinor died of a broken heart or rejection when her romance with the Wiggins boy ended.

Asa and Cora buried Elinor on Passage Key, but as the grave was discovered by Conservation officers, they demanded removal of the casket and remains. Asa, Carlos and Cora moved the remains to the old Potter's Field Cemetery on Egmont Key. They continued to live as a recluse family. Cora diligently watching her birds and insisting that Asa build bird roosts close by for her pleasure. Later Cora contracted pneumonia from exposure, passed away, and was buried at the old Potter's Field unofficial burying ground on Egmont Key near Elinor's grave.

Evidently Cora had retained some of her New Orleans dowry, which she left in its entirety to Carlos, not one farthing to Uncle Asa. Eventually, Carlos just withered away from lack of any activity, and when he joined his mother and sister in the old Egmont Key Potter's Field, what was left of his estate went to the Wiggins girl.

Uncle Asa continued to live in the bay front house with his several dogs. All slept and ate together, and as rattlesnakes or attrition took a dog or two, strays made up the difference. Uncle Asa's house had no electricity or plumbing, a pitcher pump in the yard provided cooking and drinking water, as the artesian well was a quarter mile away. There was no conventional privy. A small shack on the dock contained a two holer seat. Asa enjoyed company, but was always aware of the do-gooders who wanted to dig his mound or pirate his many marine artifacts.

Just above the high tide line of Tampa Bay, starting at Uncle Asa's door yard and extending up to Pearson Nichol's place, were intermittent clumps of giant bamboo and occasional sea grape trees. The bay breeze swaying the tall bamboo created a concert of soft musical sounds, every tone, high and low, tenor, alto and bass. This music, corded by the soft swish of waves on the bay beach, rendered a symphony beautiful beyond description. It always seemed cool and completely relaxing to sit with Uncle Asa in the shade of the big bamboo as he petted his dogs and reminisced.

The next set of ruts through the sandy woods off the north Loop Road ended at the Hickock residence on the bay. Mr. and

Off and On The Palma Sola Loop Road

Mrs. George Hickock came from the north, bought a narrow, waterfront lot from Pearson Nickols, built a little bungalow and settled down to spend their remaining days enjoying the view of Tampa Bay and the mouth of the Manatee River. Their son, Lee, had preceded them to Florida, but had settled as a fishing guide at Boca Grande, the first deep water port south of Tampa, and the most famous tarpon fishing pass in all the world, plus a luxury hotel, the "Useppa Inn", which was the spring stopover for the 1900 vintage of the "jet set." Here Lee Hickock captained the famous Hickock guide boat. To fish a tide from one of these Hickock masterpieces was the epitome of tarpon sport fishing. However, after the senior Hickock settled on Tampa Bay in Palma Sola and Lee got himself married, he moved his boat building operation to Tampa Bay and shared the bay front plot with his mother and father.

Lee's craft remained in big demand and his only helpers in construction were real craftsmen. Here Lee, his wife, and Mama and Papa Hickock lived in separate cottages. Their trips to the store and post office were sometimes weekly jaunts, but most apt to be a monthly excursion for the senior Hickocks, as Lee kept to his boat building and used water transportation to Bradenton or Tampa for supplies, and his good wife became somewhat of a recluse. When Lee met her in Boca Grande she was somewhat of an aristocratic young lady, with assets, education, position and an extensive wardrobe, which she used to the surprise and sometimes consternation of the local WCTU ladies, as she only attended the special meetings, when she was adorned in feathers and plumes, silks and satins, bustles, a high breasted corset and what-have-you.

Reached by the same sand rut road from the north Loop was the home of Pearson Nickols, his wife, Mary, and brother, Sam. Pearson and Sam were born on this site, part of the original homestead that their parents settled in the early 1880s. The original homestead was 180 acres, stretching between the mouth of the Manatee River to Seven Pines Point. The Asa Pillsbury and Hickock land were all part of the original Pearson homestead. Mother, Ann Pearson, ran a pre-school for local children in the 1880s. The school room was her attic.

After the old folks demise, Pearson and Sam maintained the small citrus grove, pastured a spavined horse for transpor-

Around the Palma Sola Loop

Nichols homestead

tation, and Pearson, the elder brother, got himself a mail-order bride, Mary.

Mary was a chubby little woman, not unattractive. She kept the house for Pearson and Sam, made her appearance at the WCTU meetings, but seldom attended church. Sam was a polio victim, had a gimpy leg and afflicted left arm, but was very sharp mentally, with piercing black eyes, a ready smile, even though there was a slight impediment of speech. Pearson was a large physical specimen, and Mary, to the consternation of certain of the WCTU ladies, readily admitted that she did everything for Sam that she did for Pearson. There were no children.

The next set of ruts meandered off the Loop Road northerly, past Zeke Routen's occasionally occupied, dilapidated, four room house on the road to Shaw's Point, which was the

Off and On The Palma Sola Loop Road

area's favorite picnic area: There was a good bay beach, clams to be dug, an old spring where Smacks stopped for good, potable water, the remains of one of the first homes on the Manatee River, and also what was left a of a huge Indian mound, made initially of shell, mostly oyster. Many of the shell roads in Manatee, Bradenton, Fogertyville and Palma Sola were paved with the shell hauled by horses, mule and wagon from this mound. Grandma Warner received a pittance from Manatee County for the privilege of leveling and hauling away the paving shell from the mound, which once had been one of the largest ceremonial Indian mounds on Florida's west coast. Shaw's Point was just another example of the desecration of most important historical sites, including Desoto's Tampa Bay landing site and main camp, the ruins of the first area post office, the old DeNoda ruins and the sweetwater spring, called Pirate's Cove spring by the Palma Sola children.

The cove behind the point was the anchorage location for the loading of the schooners that transported the Florida woods cattle to Cuba. A large holding pen, built by the local cattlemen, was located just east of the spring. The cattle were herded from this pen to the water and hoisted by the horn hump into the hold of the schooners. The majority of the cattle came from east of the Braden River, a twenty-four hour cattle drive to the Shaw's Point cattle pens.

During the Civil War there was an encampment of Confederate soldiers with lookouts from the top of the Shaw's Point shell mound, and also on the Uncle Asa ceremonial burial mound. This was part of the protection for blockade runners into the port of Tampa. Shaw's Point was later dedicated as a national park, the site of Desoto's Florida landing.

There was one other house off of this road occupied by the Glover family. The elder Glovers moved away. Papa Glover may have had an interest in the production of shine or as rumor had it, the landing of rum or red liquor.

Johnny Glover, a young man, stayed around, fished with old man Emerson at Emerson's Point, and later married Sally O'Brien, daughter of a transient produce buyer from New York. Johnny's marriage to Sally was short lived. Sally, a very pretty, well formed girl with beautiful milk and honey Irish complexion, always appeared to be right out of the tin bath

Around the Palma Sola Loop

tub, laundered and ironed. However, Sally had a vocabulary that exceeded even that of a pipe line walking dredge boat hand. Johnny later settled in Manatee and, after his second marriage became quite a favorable force in his community.

The next house up the hill was the Corker house, a two story frame, unfinished on the inside, non-descript place, with a small barn, a flowing well and a small muck land celery farm, along the drainage ditch that came from the Evans celery patch across the road. While the Corker celery farm was attended by Uncle Bill Long, the only black man in Palma Sola, the house was seldom occupied. At one interval the Lonny Smith family lived there before moving their bootlegging operation to Oneco.

There were no more residents on the north Loop Road until it ended at the Palma Sola Dock road and the Smith's "Lone Palm Brand" jelly factory. However, off to the south was Mrs. Simpson's (Pinehurst) subdivision and her ramshackled, old, two story, five room, falling apart house that she called her orphanage, and several, one, two or three room cracker shacks, vacant or occupied by drifters or field hands.

After Mr. Brooks sold his Jay Hall-share cropped farm to Mr. Ferguson, the Hall family moved into the old Simpson house in Pinehurst, selected the best soil areas and grew some prize peppers and eggplant, and a few pads of rice on the low land adjacent to the banana swamp that kept the Hall family well supplied with Ladyfingers and Horse bananas the year 'round.

* * *

The 1918 hurricane struck hard in Palma Sola. In those days the crackers would report that the Seminoles had left the 'Glades for the high land on the ridge—better batten down for a big blow. The tides covered Riverview Boulevard into Bradenton, trees were blown down across the roads. Somehow most of the shacks withstood the blow except for windows blown out and roof damage. The big old Simpson house with its add-on two story summer kitchen and upstairs sleeping

Off and On The Palma Sola Loop Road

area suffered severe damage, although Jay Hall did his best to shore up and batten down. Fish boats were washed ashore, field crops flooded out, and citrus trees stripped of leaves and green fruit. Several families holed up in the school house, and some at the store. A month later you would never know the hurricane had pruned the trees and washed the shores.

Where the east end of the north Loop Road terminates at the Palma Sola main drag, we really approach the pay dirt of old Palma Sola, starting back at the old store and post office. It was no longer Hop's store, but now under the proprietorship of Mr. and Mrs. James Jennings, who were installed as the managers of the three buildings, the store and post office, the adjacent two story rooming house, and an additional little two room cottage some two hundred feet east of the main rooming house.

The Jennings' eldest daughter had married Cordell Hull, then U.S. Secretary of State under President Wilson. Cordell was the son of Uncle Billy Hull, the Tennessee mountaineer who amassed a fortune in the lumber and land business in Tennessee. So the Jennings, Mr. and Mrs., their son, Johnny, and daughter, Katherine, both high school students, occupied the house, ran the rooming house and operated both the store and post office.

Johnny and Katherine Jennings were, for a time, not quite fully accepted by their peers in Palma Sola, but as Johnny rode his bike to high school with the others and tried out for the baseball team at school and joined in the dock swimming parties, the raids on tangerine groves and melon patches, he became one of the gang, although not completely indoctrinated in most back country ways.

Katherine was a very attractive little brunette, always aware of, and ready to exhibit, her southern aristocratic heritage, that is, generally, but some of her closest associates were aware of her willingness to, under strict security, smoke a cigarette, and otherwise be slightly risque. Both Johnny and Katherine later returned to Tennessee. Johnny became a prominent lawyer and Katherine married into a family of affluence.

Needless to say, it was quite an occasion when Secretary of State Cordell Hull or his wife visited Palma Sola. However, in

Around the Palma Sola Loop

those days the Secretary of State did not rate FBI protection, at least it was never evident when the Secretary visited the Jennings in Palma Sola.

Uncle Billy Hull, the patriarch, was short of education, but not lacking in any other respect. He had a large, unsightly bullet hole in the ridge of his nose, which caused him to squint. While in Palma Sola he roomed and had his meals at the boarding house under the management of Mrs. Jennings. He objected to any fancy foods, as he called it, and at rare intervals, when a dessert was served, he would comment that cornbread and peas was the most important vittles and was enough for anybody.

He purchased a second or third hand Maxwell and commissioned young Lester Hilliard, later of Hilliard Pontiac and Cadillac of Bradenton, to drive him on his business rounds. He insisted that Lester carry a one gallon can of gasoline, which was added to the car tank as needed, for there was no reason for gasoline in the auto tank if you were not going anywhere. Uncle Billy could write, at least enough to carry on his business. However, he always brought his letters out in plain, sealed envelopes and looked up someone, he said, who was a good writer, to "back" his letters. He dictated the name and address to the more literate person, who addressed the envelope.

Uncle Billy told a long story about how Cordell was born in a slab house at one of his back woods saw mills in Tennessee. The slab house consisted of long edge cut slabs with the outside bark left on, which were leaned in a circle around a large sweetgum tree. Of course, no floor, no windows, and usually, corn sack doors.

From the store north on the main road there were no buildings on the west side. On the east side first came the two story sand and mortar block house built by pioneer, Fred Sikes. The cement block house was built after lightening had struck his original frame house well off the road near the river and behind a small banana muck land patch. Fred Sikes and his wife were very Scotch in brogue and habit. They raised their two children, Ruby the eldest, and son Wilbur, frugally. Fred was an expert at producing charcoal. His coal mounds were placed well off in the woods where he could harvest the pine neces-

Off and On The Palma Sola Loop Road

sary to the process, and the sandy soil was right for constructing the properly ventilated mound. Beautiful foot long, two by two inch sticks were available from Mr. Sikes to charge the charcoal pots used for cooking, heating flat irons, and mosquito smudges. This was the fuel used by schooners and most small trading commercial craft for cooking. Usually the cooking fires were built in a tub of sand on the decks.

Ruby Sikes was a brilliant and witty girl, always tops at anything that she attempted. She peddled her bike to Manatee High through rain or shine, and after her graduation with honors moved to Washington, D.C., became a government girl, where she stayed until her retirement.

Wilbur Sikes, sometimes called "Whaley", worked at Ft. Dade during World War I, and, being smart and frugal, always got along. At Ft. Dade he got a soft job as deckhand on the dispatch boat that sailed into Tampa, St. Petersburg, and sometimes up the Manatee River. Wilbur always managed to have a few dollars in his pocket, had a few jobs here and there, and ended up on the Ringling yacht. His quiet, willing to work attitude attracted the attention of Mr. Ringling, so Wilbur spent some time with the circus, working up from flunky to boss of grandstand seating.

The Sike's property ran from Riverview Boulevard around the corner to the Smith property on the east Loop Road. The East Loop Road from the store to Palma Sola dock, was really main street Palma Sola. After Fred and Mother Sikes left this world, Wilbur and Ruby did not succumb to boom pressure to sell the land, but held on to all of the Palma Sola property, residence, business and waterfront.

After his circus career and World War II service experience, Wilbur moved back to Palma Sola, married Lillie Beach, the local school marm, who had earned her certificate in the late teens from the old Florida State Normal in Tallahassee. Wilbur opened a small store on the corner property, acquired the Palma Sola post office, became Postmaster and maintained the store and post office until they closed.

Adjoining the Sike's property on the north was the Frank and Katie Smith property. Facing the road was a nice three bedroom house. Frank installed carbide lights in 1915. On the north boundary was the "Lone Palm" Jelly factory. Frank

Around the Palma Sola Loop

Smith came to Florida from Georgia and met Katie on Siesta Key while he was serving as captain on one of Capt. John Fogarty's trading schooners, operating from Englewood to Tampa. Katie was the daughter of Lewis English Jay, who designed the interiors for custom finished dining and railroad private cars, working at times for both Flagler and the H.B. Plant interests. Katie's firstborn son drowned on the bay side of Siesta Key while watching his father's schooner approach from down the bay. This so disturbed Katie that she insisted on moving away from the waterfront. Thus their move to Fogertyville, where Frank built a small house and continued to operate a Fogerty line boat. While Katie lived on Siesta Key, she prepared guava jelly on her kitchen stove that was in high demand locally on Siesta Key, which even at that time had affluent residents and winter visitors.

There was never a more dedicated mother and father than Frank and Katie Smith. They moved to Palma Sola to pursue the guava jelly business seriously. Their four children inherited ambition and determination. Thelma, Furman, Carl and Ida, all had their chores around the factory, and even though neither Frank nor Katie had formal education, their ability to work, compromise and heed the advice of John T. Campbell, President of the First National Bank of Bradenton, caused them to prosper, and their private brand guava and seagrape products were soon among the delicacies served by the Pullman dining service, Charles and Co., the Waldorf Astoria, and Hotel Astor, and as many others as the supply could service.

Thelma spent two semesters at the Convent of Holy Names in Tampa and later completed training and became a graduate trained nurse. Furman left the fold for the U.S. Marines where he progressed to an honorable commission and retirement. Carl pursued his education, took a tour as a professional boxer, went into flying coastal patrol in his own aircraft during World War II, and, when Frank and Katie decided to turn over the canning factory to the kids, Carl took over. By this time the factory was also canning tomatoes in the off season.

Frank had acquired acreage around Punta Gorda to produce guavas after it seemed that climatic changes around here had made guava groves unprofitable.

Off and On The Palma Sola Loop Road

Ida and her husband took over the Punta Gorda operation, had a roadside factory, sold guava and citrus products, local candies, etc., and did well until her untimely demise when the property reverted back to the estate and Carl's management. The only scandal in the Smith family was when Carl became entangled with the IRS and Labor Relations Board. He lost his case in court after pleading his own case without professional legal assistance and served a short sentence in gentlemen's prison.

Adjoining the Smith jelly factory on the north was a grapefruit grove planted by Hal Phelps and given to his son, Clyde. This grove was never very well tended and grew the heaviest crop of maidencane of any spot in Palma Sola. Clyde's hands just did not fit a hoe.

The next house was the Frank Pillsbury home where Frank and his wife Dora, lived with their two sons. Frank also owned a truck patch down on the west fork of Warner's Bayou. Between the truck patch, his fishing and boat building, he seemed to do fairly well until Frank, who did deep free diving for lost overboard items, developed a mastoid, was rushed to Tampa by boat, too late. A sad day, Frank was a good friend to one and all in Palma Sola.

Francis and Edmond, Frank and Dora's two sons, remained around Palma Sola and helped their mother, after a very unsatisfactory second marriage, develop a local laundry, which, unfortunately, was Dora's demise, as her long hair became entangled in the mangle, where she suffocated.

The next house on the curve where the road turned to the dock was the two story bungalow home of the John Pettigrew family, John, Miss Ruby, his wife, Howard, Alice and Walter. Miss Ruby was the step-mother, John having lost his first wife shortly after Walter's birth. Mr. John was industrious and owned and operated a well drilling rig. In those days good, free flowing artesian wells were usually 5 or 6 inches in diameter, and with a head pressure that could reach the second floor of the house. Howard helped his dad on the drilling rig at times and did land improvement on the West Loop truck patch. He attended school regularly, was even allowed to drive the family Hupmobile at times, played on the Manatee High baseball team, and was the Manatee High School official artist. He was

Around the Palma Sola Loop

excellent in freehand drawing. Alice was a beautiful girl, quiet and loveable, and excellent help to Miss Ruby. Walter, a typical youngster, spent most of his time out on the dock fishing, giging, snitching, or just plain enjoying life. This family seemed to always have a bountiful table, good clothes and an automobile. Come World War I, Mr. John and Howard were immediately assigned to the Tampa Shipyard.

John Pettigrew had built a 20 by 40 foot building at the foot of the dock, which he had stated would at one time be a store. However, this never developed, and the building was used as a community club house.

Where the road obliqued east from the Pettigrew house a straight-ahead pair of sand ruts ended at the Hal Phelps home on the river bluff. Hal Phelps, a Yankee, who in the early 1890s, landed in Palma Sola, married Mamie Pillsbury, and proceeded to develop a nice home on the bluff over looking the river. Being an ardent horticulturist, Hal propagated choice mangos, grapes, guava, and even olives. His three children, Clyde, Betty and Hal, Jr., also known as PeeWee, completed the family. Clyde just missed an appointment to Annapolis and joined the Navy, Betty married a successful Manatee County School superintendent, PeeWee majored in mechanics, and later was engaged in obtaining seafood for his restaurant.

Uncle Hal, during the citrus packing season, ran the packing house on the dock, and later took over Allion's store and post office. The Hal Phelps' family seemed to have their bearings, no scandals, good concerned citizens, and were always ready with a helping hand. After World War I Clyde married Lena Rogers, a school teacher, and established a nursery on Anna Maria Island, where both Clyde and Lena became most important in island community affairs. Incidently, Mamie Phelps was the sister of Uncle Asa, Frank and Capt. Ed Pillsbury, and, of course, was the daughter of Grandpa Pillsbury, the patriarch of Palma Sola.

Further up this road and bearing to the west was the Capt. Charlie Davis home where Capt. Davis and Aunt Mary, nee Bishop, had raised their family, George, Alma, Cora, Asa and Earl. George followed the sea as an officer in the merchant marine, although he found shore time enough to woo and win Teckla Adams, daughter of Major Adams, who had developed a

Off and On The Palma Sola Loop Road

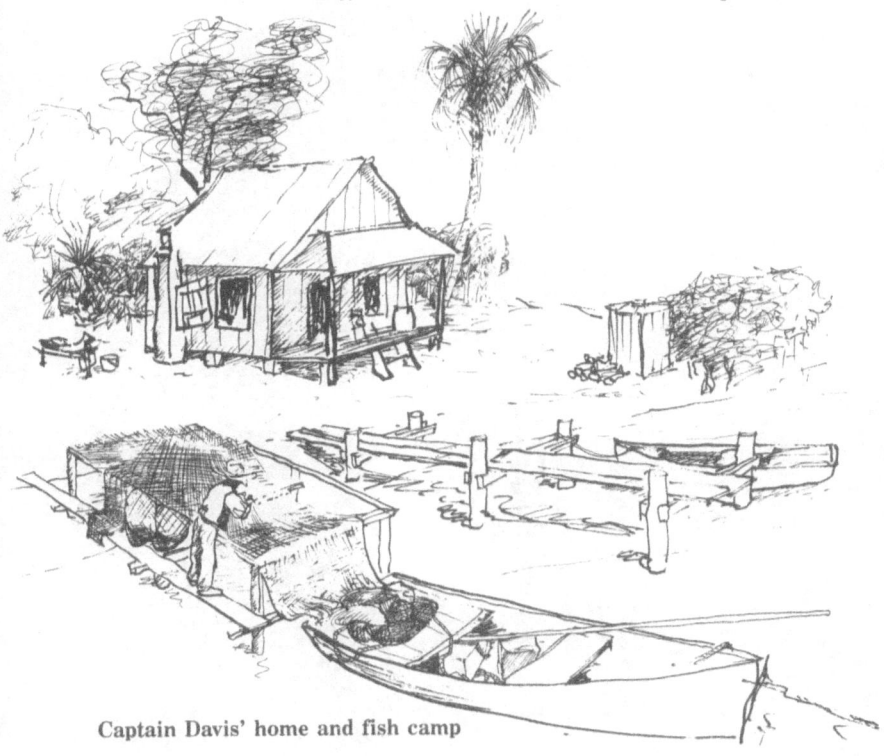

Captain Davis' home and fish camp

large plantation in old Manatee, and build the Adams' castle. The Adams' castle was headquarters for settlers during the last Indian trouble.

George and Teckla built a bungalow on the sand bluffs at Bishop Point adjacent to Capt. Davis' home on the property that was the original Bishop homestead where John Bishop raised his pioneer family prior to 1890.

Alma Davis, the older daughter, remained an old maid and spent many years at the Smith Jelly Factory. Asa Davis, a very attractive gay blade, always handy with the gals, served his stretch in the Navy, returned to the old homestead, married Lois Loggins, a local girl, raised a large family, and continued fishing and boat building, while carrying on the old Davis smoked mullet tradition of his family. Earl, the youngest son, married Rose DePrima, the daughter of an Italian lunch counter operator, who served the best hamburgers in

Around the Palma Sola Loop

Palma Sola dock

Off and On The Palma Sola Loop Road

Manatee County. Earl and Rose raised a large and productive family that scattered from St. Petersburg to Boca Grande, from water front to the woods. All were productive, some successful boat builders, others printing plant operators, commercial fishermen, and generally good business and family people. This whole area will feel the productive effects of this family for generations to come.

The last stop on the main road was a turn-around at Allion's store at the foot of the Palma Sola Dock. Mr. B.M. Allion operated a general store in a large, frame building on the waterfront. The building was originally a boat building and repair shop, operated by Asa and Frank Pillsbury. The old ways timbers remained from the waterside into the river end of the building. Mr. Allion closed the big waterside door permanently and opened a small customer entrance door on the road side. This was the only opening in the long, northwest side of the building. There were no windows, so when you entered the store it was almost totally dark, except for the back door and window back of the counter on the east side. All of the shelves were crowded with merchandise, as were most of the aisles, but Mr. Allion could lay his hands on anything in stock without delay. His cash register was a cigar box full of coins, and a square Union Leader two and a half pound tobacco tin for the paper money and charge slips.

The Allion residence was a nice cottage, a section of which was originally a small apartment type living quarters designed like the cabin of a schooner and had been the home of bachelor Asa Pillsbury, Jr. prior to his marriage. The house was set back from the road, sheltered by vegetation, where Mrs. Allion made her home, and was seldom seen, even in the yard. Her attendance at the WCTU or church services was rare. On occasion when Mr. B.M. took her to town or out for a drive in the family touring car, Mrs. Allion was seated in the rear seat with a scarf, veil and hat, alert to all the goings on, acknowledging with a smile or gesture and salute any recognition from a friend or acquaintance.

The wonderful Palma Sola dock made its landfall where the road ended adjacent to the Allion store. At the side of the dock was the Palma Sola Social Club, a 20 x 24 one room building. The citrus growers met here and, occasionally, community social meetings used the facilities. Two or three times each year a dance was held in the building. A committee, usually headed by Mrs. Ruby Pettigrew, Ruby Sikes and Katie Smith, filled and lighted the lamps and lanterns. The club Victrola, table top cranked type, was set for the music, and two or three new records were acquired for fox trot, one-step, two-step and, always, a waltz. These dances, although in the country, were not prone to promote the cracker type hoe down square dance. When the occasional demand for a "set" was made and a caller volunteered, an interim of square dancing seemed to suffice. Then back to the more popular contract foxtrots, etc. If an impromptu Thursday afternoon boatlanding or swimming party at the dock caused an unusual gathering, the key to the social hall and the Victrola were available by calling on Mrs. Ruby Pettigrew at her house just up the road. The building was owned by John Pettigrew, who had built it to house a general store in competition with Mr. Allion. For some reason the Pettigrew-Allion feud cooled down and the store never materialized, and the social club usage of the building was really a courtesy of Mr. John Pettigrew.

The Palma Sola dock, ten feet wide, was 220 feet to the channel, with one wagon turn-out on the runway. The head of the dock was covered by a citrus packing house, with adequate turn around space for the wagons which brought in the fruit and vegetables for packing. On the northwest apron was the steamboat gangplank with adequate cleats and fender piles, and also a lower mooring platform for the convenience of small craft.

The Palma Sola dock—what a marvelous place for swimming, fishing, loafing or picnicking! In those days mackerel ran rampant at the head of the dock twice a year. Red fish and trout always seemed unable to resist a hook baited with chunks of blue crab on the mossy bar halfway to shore. A couple of ladders conveniently located to climb up on the dock from the water made swimming and diving inviting.

There was nothing more conducive to community spirit, love thy neighbor, pure romance, and the real joy of being alive, than to spend time on the wonderful old Palma Sola dock and experience the soul healing effects. On and on as I traveled through the years there has been no place that created and branded the deep impressions, ideals and ambitions like the people and special places of Old Palma Sola—the store, the church, the dock.

At times of tragedy and at times of joy and celebration, this community, without a deputy sheriff, without a jail, without a reportable crime, simply bred and nurtured "Love thy neighbor". Old Palma Sola was dedicated to family and charity, and a sincere patriotism. May its spirit be perpetuated.

Epilogue

THE WARNERS

The reader of this narrative may be concerned by the mention of the Bert Warner family being the only Warner reference as we proceed around the Old Loop Road, while the story contains references to Warner's Bayou, East and West, the Warner Hotel, and Grandma Warner. The Warner family was an important factor in the development of Old Palma Sola.

Warburton A. Warner and his wife, Helen Camp Gilbert Warner settled on the Manatee River near the mouth of Warner's Bayou in the 1880's. He was a super promoter acquiring several tracts of land between the Bayou and Shaw's Point. Just West of the Bayou he built a hotel, complete with a pleasure boat dock and gazebo. A small saw mill was built on pilings near the mouth of the Bayou. The impressive 2 1/2 story Warner residence was built on the bluff east of the bayou overlooking the Manatee River, the hotel, and saw mill.

Warburton then proceeded to hob nob with the Florida and international high society including the H.B. Plant group in Tampa and the Flagler clique on the east coast while promoting Palma Sola as the fastest growing city in Florida, with unlimited opportunity for development.

In the meantime Warburton visited the Palma Sola home front at infrequent intervals to draw on the funds that his wife Helen was able to accrue from her management of the land holdings. During these visits, Warburton generated a family of three children, Gilbert, Alice, and Susan.

Later, Grandma Warner by necessity was made a "Free Dealer" by the court. She then controlled the estate, could sell, trade, mortgage or grant the properties without the approval of Warburton. However, the court directed that Warburton was to receive 50% of all net revenues.

James W. Barney, a young Kansas City Banker, recently divorced and in poor health, was lured to Palma Sola by Warburton's newspaper advertisements. He acquired a tract of land between Warner's West Bayou and the Manatee River; regained his health; wooed and wed Alice Warner; built a board and batten bungalow; experienced an unsuccessful fling at Pineapple farming, then concentrated on citrus, mangos, avocado, and honey bee cultures. He was one of the prime organizers of the Florida Citrus Exchange, and also the first President of the Florida Bee Keepers Association.

This Barney Warner union produced three children: Richard K., Janet, and John B. All three children were tutored through the third grade by Dr. (Miss) Bonell of the Dr. Parker clan. They then attended the Palma Sola rural grade school prior to attending Manatee High in Bradenton. The Barney family's only activity in old Palma Sola was the childrens' two and a half mile trek up the shell road to the Palma Sola rural school.

Richard K. (Dick) had a fling at college in Gainesville, was a confidant to the Ringling family, and did well in business. Janet concentrated on Community projects, married Willis Hampton and later fell heir to Grandma Warner's home where she still resides. John completed his engineering studies and later returned to Palma Sola for a stormy experience in real estate development which was cut short by his early demise.

Susan Warner the youngest child of the Warburton and Helen union, waited until middle life to marry Harry Tallent, a Palma Sola truck farmer. They built a cottage next to Grandma Warner's as their permanent home. They had no children.

The whole Warner clan except Bert, and especially the Barney branch, was by most Palma Solians considered "Upper Crust". They had their mail come R.F.D. Bradenton, attended church in Bradenton, and traded at Mowers Fancy Grocery and Western Meats. The kids even wore shoes to the Palma Sola School.

THE FELTSES

Jim Felts and his first wife, Rosie Nancy Barksdale, had six children; the eldest, Gratton Hugh, was followed by Letha L., Tressa Vera, Mary Alice, Carl Fabin, and Ross Barksdale. Mother Rosie passed away the day Ross was born. All six children spent their youth in Palma Sola at the homestead on the west Loop Road.

Four years after Rosie's passing, Jim married Idell Prince and proceeded to produce a second family of nine children. They were William Franklin, Buelah E., James Wilken, Idell, Otis Gates, Herman Alonzo, Helen, Charles Claton, and Princie Ella. Any attempt to follow the fifteen Felts children would be a volume of adventure through three wars, with brothers sticking together from Alaska to Korea and all points in between.

PALMA SOLA LOOP ROAD TODAY (1986)

East Loop is 70th Street NW

North Loop is 17th Avenue NW

West Loop is 99th Street NW

South Loop is 9th Avenue NW

Riverview Boulevard converts to 15th Avenue NW at 70th Street NW

Map of Old Palma

TAMPA BAY

Smith's Bayou

LEE HICKOCK BOAT WORKS

NICHOLS HOMESTEAD

TRAIL TO SEVEN PINES AND RUINS

ASA PILLSBURY JR. HOME AND MANGO GROVE

HICKOCK HOME

Seven Pines Point

JIM FELTS HOME AND FARM

RUDE TRUCK FARM AND HOME

DEACON ROGERS HOME

SCHO

ROSS FELTS FARM

E. T. MOORE SHACK

SMITH'S GUAVA GROVE

CHARLES PETTIGREW HOUSE

C. H. BRADLEY HOME

GRANDPA PILLSBURY HOME AND DOCK

TOLAND HOME

Palma Sola Bay

About the Author

Fred L. Hall was born in Smithville, Missouri, on November 2nd, 1902. His family went to Bisbee Territory of Arizona in 1907, then on to Manatee County, Florida, in 1913. Manatee County was sparsely settled in 1913. These were truly pioneer days in this part of the world. Fred's education was sparse as schools were scarce in these days. He attended the intermediate grades at the Palma Sola rural school, and later subscribed to correspondence courses and attended night school when work assignments permitted.

At age 13, he started working as a laborer, deck hand, and chauffeur. Later, the Florida real estate boom made capitalists out of many ambitious Cracker youths. He joined the rush to riches, only to return to the ranks of the hungry and broke when the boom busted in 1925.

He succeeded in landing a job in Pittsburgh. There, he managed to stay clear of unions, worked hard, and was rewarded with some success. During WWII he was appointed a "technical advisor" to the Chief of Ordinance where he reported to the Pentagon on classified assignments. After VJ day, he returned to industry, but maintained family headquarters in Florida while completing executive sales assignments at Bendix, Fruehauf, and Mercury Outboards. Fred finally retired from Grumann Allied Industries as sales manager.

In 1966, he again became a Manatee County full-timer. Here he managed the Marine Industries Association of Manatee and Sarasota counties and produced the Florida Suncoast Boat Shows. He became known in local political circles as "Boat Ramp Hall" because of his efforts to have county boat ramps built for trailer boats. He and his wife, Kathryn, are now residents of Palmetto, Florida.

ISBN 0-8200-1033-2

www.ingramcontent.com/pod-product-compliance
Lightning Source LLC
Chambersburg PA
CBHW031429290426
44110CB00011B/587